I0119529

Samuel Warren

A manual of elementary problems in the linear perspective of form and shadow

In two parts

Samuel Warren

A manual of elementary problems in the linear perspective of form and shadow
In two parts

ISBN/EAN: 9783337276249

Printed in Europe, USA, Canada, Australia, Japan

Cover: Foto ©Andreas Hilbeck / pixelio.de

More available books at **www.hansebooks.com**

INDUSTRIAL SCIENCE DRAWING.

A MANUAL

OF

ELEMENTARY PROBLEMS

IN THE

LINEAR PERSPECTIVE

OF

𝔉𝔬𝔯𝔪 𝔞𝔫𝔡 𝔖𝔥𝔞𝔡𝔬𝔴;

OR THE

REPRESENTATION OF OBJECTS AS THEY APPEAR,

MADE FROM THE

REPRESENTATION OF OBJECTS AS THEY ARE

In Two Parts.

PART I.—PRIMITIVE METHODS; WITH AN INTRODUCTION.

PART II.—DERIVATIVE METHODS; WITH SOME NOTES ON AERIAL PERSPECTIVE.

By S. EDWARD WARREN, C. E.,

PROFESSOR OF DESCRIPTIVE GEOMETRY, ETC., IN THE RENSSELAER POLYTECHNIC INSTITUTE
AND AUTHOR OF THE "DRAFTSMAN'S MANUAL;" AND "GENERAL PROBLEMS OF
DESCRIPTIVE GEOMETRY."

NEW YORK:

JOHN WILEY & SONS,

15 ASTOR PLACE.

1888.

Entered according to Act of Congress, in the year eighteen hundred and sixty-three, by

S. EDWARD WARREN,

In the Clerk's Office of the District Court of the United States for the Northern District of
New York.

CONTENTS.

PAGE

PREFACE .... - vi

INTRODUCTION.

CHAPTER I.—*Instruments and Materials*............................. 9

   Paper... 9

   Support of Paper 9

   Pencils... 9

   Rulers.. 9

   Compasses........ 10

   Use of Compasses.................................. 10

   Irregular Curves 10

   Indian Ink.. 10

CHAPTER II.—*Preliminary Principles and Explanations*............... 12

PART I.

PRIMITIVE METHODS.

CHAPTER I.—*Definitions and General Principles*................... 1

  " II.—*The Elements of Projections*........................... 1

  " III.—*The Construction of the Perspectives of Objects from their Projections*....................................... 24

  " IV.—*Real Projections, and Perspectives made from them*.......... 28

   Perspectives of Geometrical Solids, Art. (68.)........... 32

   Example 1.—To Find the Perspective of a Vertical Square Prism.. °2

    " 2.—To Find the Perspective of a Triangular Pyramid....... 35

PAGE

CHAPTER V —*Removal of Practical Difficulties, arising from the confusion of Projections and Perspectives.* 36

§ I. —*First Method.*—Translation forward of the Perspective Plane.. 36

    Example 3.—To Find the Perspective of a Cube, etc. 38

§ II.—*Second Method.*—Use of Three Planes. 38

    Example 4.—To Find the Perspective of an Obelisk, etc. ... 41

VI.—*Projections and Perspectives of Circles, and of Bodies having partly or wholly curved boundaries.* 4

    Example 5.—To Find the Perspective of a Circle, lying in the horizontal plane. 43

        Of Planes, Arts. (77–84.). 45–46

    "   6.—To Find the Perspective of a Cylinder, standing on the horizontal plane. 47

    "   7.—To Find the Perspective of a Cone, standing on the horizontal plane. 50

    "   8.—Do. of a Cone whose axis is parallel to the ground line. 52

    "   9.—Do. of a Cone whose axis is parallel to the vertical plane only. 54

    "   10.—Do. of a Cone whose axis is oblique to both planes of projection. 55

    "   11.—To Find the Perspective of a Sphere. 58

        First Method of finding the apparent contour. 58

        Second Method   "   "   " 61

    "   12.—To Find the Perspective of a Concave Cupola Roof. 63

CHAPTER VII.—*Perspectives of Shadows* 65

    General Principles and Illustrations, Arts. (89–99.). 65

    Example 13.—To Find the Perspective of the Shadow of a Square Abacus on a Square Pillar. 67

    "   14.—Do. of a Triangular Pyramid upon the Horizontal Plane. 69

    "   15.—Do. of a Dormer Window upon a Roof. 71

PART II.

DERIVATIVE METHODS.

CHAPTER I.—*General Principles and Illustrations.* 75

    Example 1.—To Find the Vanishing Point of Telegraph Wires, etc. 78

PAGE

Example 2.—To Find the Vanishing Point of a Perpendicular and of a Diagonal............... 79

Particular Derivative Methods, Arts. (118–121.) 81

" 3.—To Find the Perspective of a Straight Line, in any position oblique to both planes of projection, etc. 82

" 4.—Do. of a Tower and Spire................. 84

Practical Remarks, Art. (122.) 86

" 5.—To Find the Perspective of a Cross and Pedestal 89

CHAPTER II.—*Perspectives of Shadows*........................... .. 92

Example 6.—To Find the Vanishing Point of Rays, and of their Horizontal Projections 92

" 7.—To Find the Perspective of the Shadow of any Vertical Line upon the Horizontal Plane. 93

CHAPTER III.—*Miscellaneous Problems*................................. 96

Example 8.—To Find the Perspective of a Pavement of Squares, whose sides are parallel to the ground line............... 96

" 9.—Do. of a Pavement of Hexagons, whose sides make angles of 30° and 90° with the ground line 98

" 10.—Do. of an Interior........................ 98

" 11.—Do. of the Shadows in an Interior.......... 102

" 12.—Do. of a Cabin 104

" 13.—Do. of the Shadow of a Chimney on a Roof.. 108

CHAPTER IV.—*Pictures, and Aerial Perspective*........................... 110

Landscape Outlines..................................... 110

Landscape Details.—Trees........................... 111

Hills 111

Valleys........................... 111

Ascent and Descent....... 112

Level of the Eye.................. 112

Reflections in Water............... 113

Location of the Centre of the Picture. 113

Do. of the Perspective Plane........ 114

Shadows of Trees, and other Vertical Objects 114

Time of a Given Aspect............ 114

Light and Shade 115

Edges 116

Color............................. 116

PREFACE.

FOR several years past, while teaching a comparatively advanced course on Perspective, embracing some of its higher problems, I have cherished a purpose to compose an elementary perspective, for general use; which should be clearly demonstrative at every step, and also, if possible, interesting to its readers; which should, in fact, be truly popular, without being empirical; and, on the other hand, perfectly demonstrative, without being too elevated. In other words, I have sought to make my work elementary, not in the sense of merely stating perspective facts without adequate explanation, but in the sense of selecting simple, yet widely and always useful examples, and then fully explaining, in easy order, the few plain principles necessary to the solution of such examples.

An exact knowledge of perspective is *indispensable* to those who would make exact representations, for industrial purposes, of architectural or mechanical structures as they *appear*. It is *highly useful* to those, even, who practise perspective as an ornamental art, in the making of pictures; inasmuch as it enables them to *know* scientifically, as well as *feel* sensibly, whether their drawings are correct or incorrect. It is also *interesting* to the amateur judges and admirers of pictures, as well as to their makers; and, finally, it is *useless to none* who are in any manner engaged with *the arts of graphical representation or design*.

It is a part of *the price of truth*, whereby we discover its worth, that we must discover the truth *concerning propriety of arrangement* in any subject, as an indispensable condition for its successful treatment. A course of research, which in any degree ignores certain elements on which it is based, cannot but become proportionately involved in bewildering, and, both to the student and critic, comfortless confusion and intricacy. It is equally true, that natural progress from a proper starting point cannot fail to be effectual and agreeable.

As the truth about primary industrial utilities for daily working life, is more elementary and fundamental than truth about beauty and other higher utilities for the adornment of higher life, it results, in the present instance, that "Projections," which, usually for industrial purposes, represent objects as they *are*, in form and size, naturally precede, in a course of exact study, "Perspective," which, usually for pictorial effect, represents objects as they *appear*.

Perspectives, or drawings of objects as they *appear*, are made, then, from *Projections*, or drawings of objects as they *are;* and which, therefore, are competent representatives of those objects.

The study of projections thus properly preceding that of perspective, as its natural foundation, disadvantages will unavoidably arise from attempts to treat of exact perspective, without a formal preliminary treatment of projections. Hence, this work, while complete in itself, is the natural successor, for those who use both, of my "Manual of Elementary Geometrical Drawing of Three Dimensions," in which objects are shown in projection only.

It is unfortunate for learners, that a subject so simple, useful, and attractive, as Perspective is, when properly treated, should come to be regarded with aversion, merely owing to defects in its treatment; the chief of which defects is, perhaps, the failure fully to exhibit its foundation in "projections."

The present volume is an attempt to expressly present Perspective, as founded on "Projections," and in this respect it differs, more or less noticeably, from numerous elementary works on the subject. I accordingly hope for such results, in respect to ready and interested understanding of the subject, as the improved treatment of it, which I have endeavored to give, leads me to anticipate.

The construction of the perspective of a shadow is, from first to last, a problem of more tediousness and complexity, espe cially as applied to complex objects and positions, than falls within the scope of an elementary work like the present. Hence, only a few, and quite simple, problems in perspectives of shadows have been inserted.

The simplest conception, and resulting definition, of the perspective of a point is, that it is where the "visual ray" through the point pierces the plane of the picture, *i.e.* the "perspective plane."

The method of construction just indicated, and here adopted for PART I., does away with the whole machinery of "vanishing points," "perpendiculars," "diagonals," etc.; and, accordingly, these, with their advantages, are briefly explained and illustrated, in PART II., as incidental matters, giving rise to derivative methods of construction, and tending to aid the reader in understanding the methods usually employed by writers on perspective.

In a proposed future general work on perspective, I hope to exhibit more fully a systematic arrangement of all its methods. and interesting peculiarities and details.

UNIVER
A.. RN.

LINEAR PERSPECTIVE.

INTRODUCTION.

CHAPTER I.

INSTRUMENTS AND MATERIALS.

1. PAPER.—For elementary practice, thick unruled writing, or tough printing paper, will answer. For nicer work, German cartoon, or English smooth drawing paper, will be convenient; and for exact constructions, in lines or tints of Indian Ink, Whatman's drawing paper will be best.

2. *Support of the Paper.*—For slight pencil or ink sketches, the paper may lie flat on an atlas, or a few thicknesses of smooth paper, or any firm, but not rigid surface. For larger and exact ink drawings, the paper must be well wet, and then fastened round the edges with gum-arabic, to a smooth board. Then, when dry, it will be found to be tightly stretched.

Great care should be taken to keep paper flat and smooth, when not stretched as just described.

3. PENCILS.—For sketching, use a hard pencil, as No. 4, or 5, of Faber's, and make only the faintest lines. For finishing up pencil drawings, use softer and blacker pencils, as No. 3 for well defined objects, and Nos. 1 and 2 for shadows, foliage, &c.

In pencilling a drawing which is to be inked, use a pencil sharpened on a fine file, to a thin edge, rather than a round point, since it will thus keep sharp much longer.

4. RULERS.—For drawing on stretched paper, use a T rule, for drawing all lines from right to left; and a right angled triangle, for drawing lines perpendicular to these. With loose paper, use a common ruler and right angled triangle.

5. *To draw parallels in any oblique position,* by a ruler and tri angle. To draw through *p*, for example, a parallel to *ab*. Place

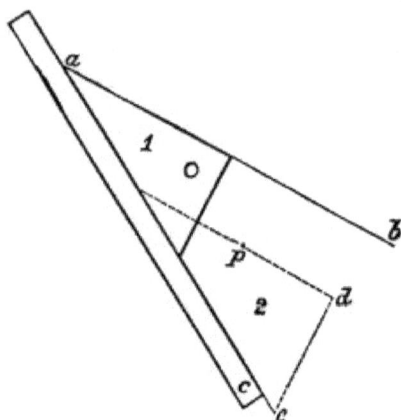

FIG. 1.

a side of the triangle on *ab*, and bring up the ruler *ac*, as shown in Fig. 1. Hold the ruler fast, and slide down the triangle to the position (2) when *pd* will be parallel to *ab*.

6. *To draw perpendiculars in oblique positions.*—Slide the triangle, as before, till *de* passes through *p*, then *d* being a right angle, a line can be drawn through *p*, and perpendicular to *ab*.

7. COMPASSES.—For drawing ink or pencil circles, the compasses should have movable legs, which may be replaced by a drawing pen, or pencil-holder.

8. *In using the compasses,* hold them by the joint, with the thumb and forefinger. Then, in setting off distances on a line, turn them, alternately, on one side and the other of the line, never taking both points at once from the paper, till the operation is finished. This method is most expeditious and accurate. Like wise, in describing a circle, the whole can be accomplished with quick and uninterrupted motion.

9. *Irregular Curves.*—For drawing other curves than circles, points of which have been previously constructed, use the thin plate of wood with variously curved edges and openings, and called an irregular curve.

10. INDIAN INK.—This color, when of good quality, is of a brownish black, and is prepared in polished or gilded cakes, fine-grained, and usually scented with musk or camphor. It is prepared for use, like other water colors, by touching the end to water, and

rubbing on an earthen plate or tile. When enough has been ground off, wipe the cake dry to prevent its crumbling.

11. This ink, when thick, may be applied in a drawing-pen, or brush, so as to make black lines, or surfaces. When diluted with a quantity of water, tints of any degree of lightness may be quickly laid on the paper (stretched) by a rapid use of a goose-quill sized, or larger camel's hair brush.

CHAPTER II.

PRELIMINARY PRINCIPLES AND EXPLANATIONS.

12. Sitting by a window, you may fix your attention on all that you see through one of its panes—buildings and parts thereof, trees, roads, fields, woods, streams and clouds.

As soon, however, as you give attention, *both* to the pane and to what you see through it, you will find that, by looking with each eye separately, you will see partly different sights through the same pane. Hence, to see definitely both the pane and what you see through it, you must close one eye.

13. This being done, you might paint upon the glass everything that you see through it, just where you see it, and of the same shade and color. A perfect picture, in every respect, of all seen through the glass, from one point of sight, might thus be made on the pane. Such a picture would be called the *perspective* of the view seen through the pane.

14. I. Hence a *perspective* is a picture which shows one or more objects just as they appear, in respect both to form and color, and as seen from one fixed point of sight.

15. If seated quite near the window, you will observe that you cannot see all that is to be seen through it, without turning the head; while each new direction of sight gives you at least a partly new view. Also each new position of the eye gives, evidently, a different view through the same pane.

16. II. Hence any single perspective drawing should embrace no more than one view, that is, no more than can really be seen when *looking in one direction from one fixed point of sight.*

17. The chief exceptions to this rule are in panoramic and architectural interior scene painting, which, being intended to please large assemblies, are painted from several points of sight, or from one quite remote one.

18. All this being understood, suppose you are in a field, and viewing a distant tree through a framed pane of glass, held at a fixed distance from the eye. As you approach the tree it appears to occupy a larger and larger portion of the glass; while, as you recede from it, a contrary effect is produced.

III. Hence the size of the object, *in a picture*, depends on its distance from the eye.

19. Again; if your distance from the tree is fixed, the nearer the pane is carried to the tree the more completely will the view of the tree fill it. That is—

IV. The comparative size of an *object* in the picture, and the *whole* picture, depends also on the distance of the picture plan from the object.

20. Further, if two trees, at equal distances, and of different sizes, be viewed at once through the same pane, and from the same fixed position, the larger one will cover a larger space on the pane, as seen through it.

V. Hence, other things being the same, the size of an object, in the picture, depends on its actual size.

21. Once more, by moving, together with the pane, from side to side, or up and down, the tree will be seen through different portions of the pane, when seen from the different positions so taken.

VI. That is, the place of an object in a given picture, its size and distance being also given, depends on its direction from the observer.

22. VII. From the last four particulars, we now conclude that, in order to represent a given object truly, its *dimensions, distance from the picture, distance from the eye, and direction* must all be known.

In other words, the *relative position* of the *eye*, the *picture*, and the *object*, and the *size of the latter*, must be known.

23. Returning now to the picture painted on the window pane, each point of that picture is in a straight line, from the point represented, to the eye. Such a line is called a *visual ray*.

VIII. Hence the perspective of any point is where the visual ray from that point meets the surface of the picture.

Finally, the following general principles may serve to connect his introductory sketch, which embraces the primary facts of perspective, given by the testimony of the senses, with the more exact treatment of the subject, which succeeds, and in which the principles of perspective, based upon these facts, are demonstrated.

24. Science is a complete body of truth, whose parts are naturally related to each other; and hence may be expressed by a systematic and connected statement of successive particulars, proceeding in natural order from primary elements to complete results.

Perspective science is such a body of truth, relating to the manner of representing objects as they appear. This science is founded on the simple facts of vision already described, and which are learned by observing *what* and *how* we see.

As in making a picture itself, its outlines and most conspicuous objects, alone, may be represented, or all its peculiarities and details may also be included; so a science may be presented in its outlines only, or in entire completeness.

This work aims to exhibit little more than the outlines of the subject of perspective, but yet fully enough to assist any one, who desires to draw ordinary objects as a business or pleasure, to do so intelligently and accurately.

We now proceed to unfold the elements of Perspective from the preceding simple facts of vision, and to apply those elements to practical exercises in perspective drawing.

PART I.

PRIMITIVE METHODS.

CHAPTER I.

DEFINITIONS AND GENERAL PRINCIPLES.

25. The complete perspective of an object, is a picture of it, which, when viewed from a certain point, produces the same image upon the eye that the object itself does, when viewed from the same point.

Each point and line of such a picture, must, when suitably placed between the eye and the object, exactly cover and conceal from view the corresponding points and lines of that object. It must also, as truly as art will allow, present, at each point, the same shade and color that is exhibited by the same object.

26. Hence perspective embraces two branches: the perspective of *form*, called *linear perspective ;* and the perspective of *color and gradations of shade*, called *aerial perspective*.

27. Aerial perspective is an *imitative art*, founded on extensive observation of nature, and on the science of optics.

Linear perspective is either an imitative art, or an art of exact geometrical construction, according as the outlines of pictures of given objects are traced by the eye, or constructed with instruments, according to geometrical principles.

28. In point of fact, linear perspective is practised as a *constructive* art, chiefly in its application to *regular objects*. It is practised as an *imitative* art, mainly in the drawing of irregular, or picturesque objects, such as trees, animals, hills, streams, and old buildings.

We will next inquire into the natural principles, which lead to the exact construction of the perspectives of objects.

29. The eyes are so related, that in attempting to see, with both of them together, objects at different instances, distinctly and at once, we see these objects partly double (12).

Hence in making an exact picture of any object, we suppose it

to be viewed with one eye, or that the two eyes are reduced to a
single seeing point, called the *point of sight* (14).

30. Objects become visible by means of rays of light, reflected
from them to the eye, and called *visual rays* (23).

31. Rays of light proceed in straight lines; as is proved by the
fact that we can see nothing through an opaque bent tube.

32. The visible boundary of an object is called its *apparent contour.* The perspective of this contour, is the *linear perspective* of
the object.

33. Any body, having a vertex, and plane sides, is, in a genera'
sense, called a *Pyramid.*

Any curved surface, having a vertex, and therefore containing
straight lines drawn through that vertex, is a *Cone*, in the general
sense of the term.

Hence visual rays, from all points of the apparent contour of an
object to the eye, form a *pyramid*, or a *cone*—whose vertex is the
point of sight—according as the object is bounded by *straight* or
by *curved* lines. This being understood, this pyramid and cone
are, for the sake of brevity, called indifferently the *visual cone.*

34. Next, conceive a plane to intersect the visual cone, anywhere
between its vertex, that is the eye, and its base, that is the object.
This plane will cut from the cone a figure which will exactly conceal
from the eye at its vertex, the apparent contour of the original
object. That is (25) this figure will be the linear perspective (27)
of that contour, and hence of the object (32).

35. In like manner, the intersection of the visual ray (23) from
any one point of the given object, with the given plane, is the
perspective of the point from which that ray proceeded.

36. The given plane is therefore called the *perspective plane;*
and is understood to be vertical, unless the contrary is mentioned.

Illustration.—In Fig. 2, let E be the position of the eye, ABC
the object, as a wood or paper triangle, to be represented; and PQ,
the perspective plane. Then AE, BE, and CE, represent visual
rays from the corners or vertices of the given triangle. Now let
a, *b*, and *c* represent the points in which these visual rays pierce
the perspective plane PQ, then *abc* will be the perspective of ABC.

37. It now clearly appears, that, in order to find the perspective
of an object, three things must be given; *the object* itself, the position of *the eye*, and *the perspective plane* (22). Observe here, also,
that, as lines from the visible points of the object to the eye are
visual rays, these rays become known as soon as the positions of the
eye and of the object are given.

If either of the lines, as *ab*, of the perspective, were prolonged either way, or both ways, it would be called the *indefinite perspective* of the original line as AB.

38. Any angle, as AEC, formed at the eye by two visual rays

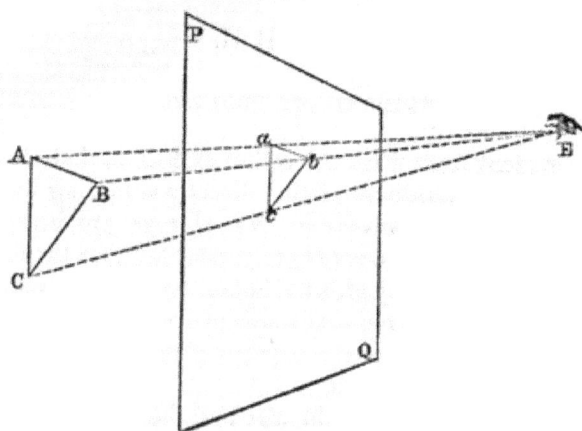

FIG. 2.

is called a *visual angle*. It now appears that any line, as AC, and its perspective, *ac*, subtend the same visual angle. The reason, therefore, why an object and its perspective present the same appearance (25) to the eye, is, that they subtend the same visual angle; for the apparent size of any object depends on the size of the visual angle which includes it. Hence if two equal lines be in parallel positions, but at unequal distances from the eye, the further one will subtend the smaller visual angle and will therefore appear the shorter (18). Also, if a line or a surface be viewed obliquely, instead of directly, it will appear of diminished size, and is said to be *foreshortened*.

39. The position, E, of the eye, and the form and position of the bject ABC remaining fixed, there will be as many different *sizes* and *forms* of the perspective, *abc*, as there may be different distances and positions of the perspective plane, between E and ABC And these various forms and sizes of *abc* will all be true perspectives of ABC. To understand this completely, it is only necessary to remember, 1°: That all these forms of *abc* are sections of the same visual pyramid ABC—E (34), and 2°: That the definition of a perspective is *not*, a figure that *is* as the original object appears; but, only, one that *appears* as that object does, when viewed from the same point (25).

2

CHAPTER II.

THE ELEMENTS OF PROJECTIONS.

40. It is evident from a consideration of Fig. 2, that we cannot, practically, find a perspective picture directly according to (35) *i. e.* directly from objects themselves. Visual rays are invisible and intangible, and we cannot conveniently substitute for them, threads from every point of an object, as a house, to a fixed point, as the top of a stake, taken to represent the place of the eye, and then find where all the threads pierce a paper plane, set up between the object and the place of the eye.

41. What then *can* be used in place of the actual object, from which to make its perspective, as truly as if found mechanically, as above described? We employ auxiliary drawings, which show the positions, forms, and dimensions of the original objects, just as they really *are*, and from such drawings, with similar representations of the visual rays, we construct the perspectives, which show those objects as they *appear.*

42. These auxiliary drawings, which show the given object, and its visual rays, as they really *are*, in respect to form and relative position, are called *projections.* To the explanation and construction of projections, we therefore turn, as the next thing in order.

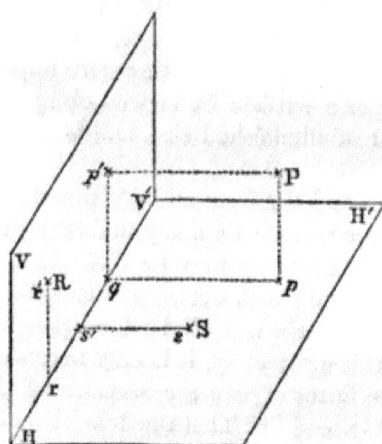

FIG. 3.

43. *Illustration.* — Let HH', Fig. 3, represent a level plane, called the *horizontal plane*, and VV' an upright plane, at right angles to HH', and hence called the *vertical plane.*

The floor and any wall of a room, would be such a horizontal and vertical plane. HV', the intersection of these planes, is called the *ground line.*

Next, let P be any point in the open angular space between these two planes. Then let Pp be a straight line from P, perpendicular to the horizontal plane, HH', and meeting it at some point represented by p. Likewise, let Pp' be a line from P, perpendicular to the vertical plane, VV', and meeting it at p'. Then P is called the *horizontal projection* of P, and p' is the *vertical projection* of P.

44. Observe now, according to (41) that the two projections of a point are an adequate representative of the real position of the point. For $p'q$, the vertical height of the vertical projection, p', above the ground line HV', is equal to the real height, Pp, of the point P above the horizontal plane. Likewise pq, the perpendicular distance of the horizontal projection, p, from the ground line, is equal to the real distance, Pp', of the point in space, P, from the vertical plane. Hence *a point is named by naming its projections;* thus, we describe P as the point pp'.

45. If a point, as S, is in the horizontal plane, it coincides with its horizontal projection, s, and its vertical projection, s', must be in the ground line HV'. Likewise, if a point, as R, lies in the vertical plane, it is its own vertical projection, r', and its horizontal projection, r, must be in the ground line.

46. By considering the explanations just given, we are led to the following additional practical particulars. *First:* The *forms* of bodies are indicated by the positions of the points which compose or limit their bounding lines. Hence, if the distinguishing points of the boundaries of an object be projected in the simple manner just explained, and if the projections of these points be connected, in each plane, the projections of the object will be formed. *Second:* p represents the real point, P, as it would appear if seen from above, in the vertical direction Pp. Likewise p' represents the same point as seen in looking in the direction Pp'. *Third:* In order to view all the points of an object simultaneously in the sam direction, the eye must be at an indefinitely great distance from it Hence projections represent objects as they *would* appear, if visible from an indefinitely great distance, and viewed in a direction perpendicular to each plane of projection in succession.

47. *Illustration.* Fig. 4. GL is the ground line; GH, the horizontal plane ; and GV, the vertical plane. ABC–D is a triangular prism, placed with its edges parallel to the ground line. In viewing this prism from a great distance above it, so as to look at all parts at once, in the parallel directions Aa, Ff, &c., the two sloping

sides, ACDF and ABDE, will be visible. Projecting the corners of these faces by vertical projecting lines, Aa, &c., as in Fig. 3, we find *acfd* for the horizontal projection of ACFD, and *abde* for the horizontal projection of ABDE.

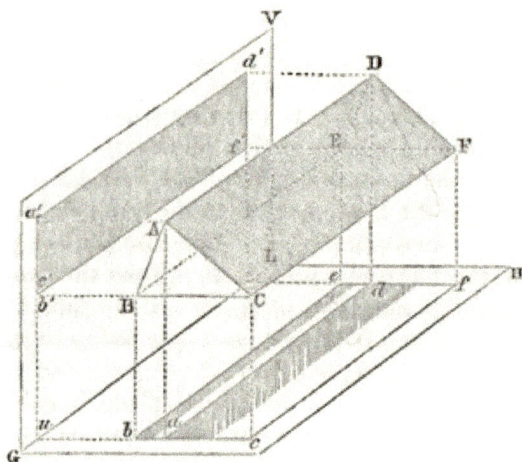

Fig. 4.

Likewise, in viewing the prism in the direction Aa', its front, ACDF, only, is visible, and $a'c'd'f'$ is the vertical projection of this face.

It thus appears that the horizontal projection shows the true relative distances of all points of the prism, front of the vertical plane ; and that the vertical projection shows the true heights of all points of the prism above the horizontal plane. That is, the two projections, together, form an adequate representative of the form of the prism.

48. In particular, the face BCEF is parallel to the horizontal plane, and $bcef$, its horizontal projection, is equal to it. That is, *when a surface, or line, is parallel to a plane of projection, its true size is shown in its projection upon that plane.* Again, CB is a line which is perpendicular to the vertical plane, and hence the point c' is its vertical projection. That is, *when a line is perpendicular to either plane of projection, its projection on that plane is a point.*

49. Continuing to examine this figure, 4, with reference, now, to its lines only, it appears that CF, for example, is parallel to both planes of projection, and hence to the ground line, and its projections cf and $c'f'$ are both parallel to the ground line, and each

equal to CF. That is, *when a line is parallel to the ground line, each of its projections is parallel to the ground line, and equal to the line.*

50. Again : AC, for example, is oblique to both planes of projection, but it is in a plane A*a'uc*, which is perpendicular to both of these planes, and both of its projections, *ca* and *c'a'*, are perpendicular to the ground line, and each is less than the line AC. That is, *when any line is oblique to both planes of projection, and is in a plane perpendicular to both, each of its projections is less than the line, and is perpendicular to the ground line.*

51. In Fig. 5, AB is a line which is parallel to the horizontal plane GH, only. *ab* and *a'b'* are its projections. *ab*=AB, and *a'b'* is less than AB and parallel to the ground line. That is, *when a line is parallel to the horizontal plane only, its horizontal projection is equal and parallel to itself, and its vertical projection is parallel to the ground line and less than the line itself.*

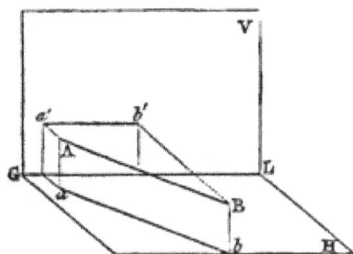

FIG. 5.

52. In Fig. 6, AB is a line parallel only to the vertical plane VL, *ab*, its horizontal projection, is parallel to GL, and less than AB. *a'b'*, its vertical projection, is equal and parallel to AB. That is, *when a line is parallel to the vertical plane only, its vertical projection is equal and parallel to the line, and its horizontal projection is parallel to the ground line, and less than the given line.*

53. Finally, in Fig. 7, AB is a line which is oblique to both planes of projection. Each of its projections, *ab* and *a'b'*, is less than AB, and oblique to GL. That is, *when a line is oblique to both planes of projection, both of its projections are less than itself, and are oblique to the ground line.* Article 50 is a special case of this principle.

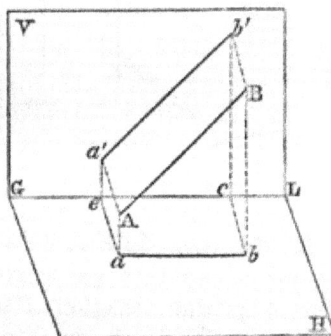

FIG. 6.

If lines, in any position, are parallel, their projections will be parallel.

Lines, like points, are, in the language of projections, named by naming their projections (44). Thus, in the three preceding figures, the line itself, AB, would be designated as the line *ab–a'b'*, the vertical projection being distinguished by accents.

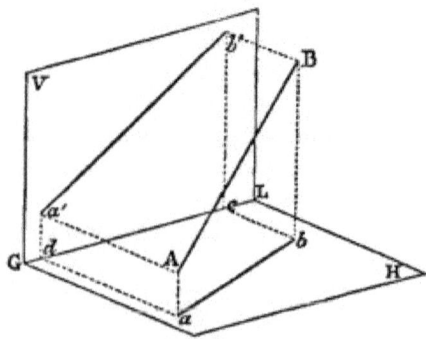

54. The space on the same side of the vertical, or perspective plane, as the eye, is said to be in front of it. If, now, the horizontal plane, GII, be extended back of the vertical plane CV, Fig. 4, an angular space in which objects may be placed, will be formed behind the vertical plane.

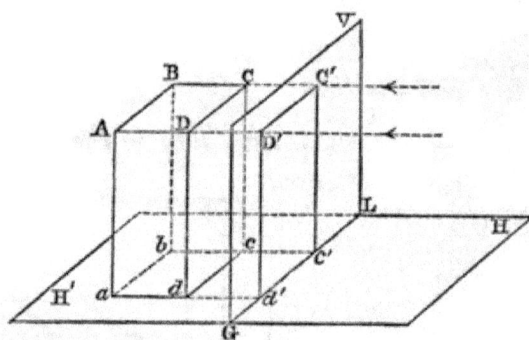

FIG. 7.

angular space in which objects may be placed, will be formed behind the vertical plane.

FIG. 8.

Illustration.—In Fig. 8, let GH be the front part of the horizontal plane, and GH' its back part—the vertical plane, GV, being viewed in the direction of the arrows. Let AC*bd* be a square prism standing on the back part of the horizontal plane, and with its faces parallel and perpendicular to the vertical plane. Then, as shown in the figure, C'D'*c'd'*, a rectangle, equal to the face CD*cd*, will be the vertical projection of this prism, and its lower base, *abcd*, will constitute its horizontal projection.

Observe, here, that when a body stands on the horizontal plane, its vertical projection will stand on the ground line.

Remarks.—a. In practice, and for brevity, the horizontal projection is called the *plan*, and the vertical projection, the *eleva-tion*.

b. If, in the three preceding figures, the given lines had been placed *behind* the vertical plane, their vertical projections would have remained the same, and their horizontal projections would have appeared behind the ground line, and parallel to their present positions. The student is recommended to reconstruct these figures accordingly.

55. In (41) projections were spoken of as drawings which show objects as they *are*, rather than as they *appear*. That is, projections show the real forms and dimensions of objects. This will now appear from a fuller examination of Figs. 4 and 8. In Fig. 4, the prism being placed with its length parallel to the ground line, and one of its rectangular faces parallel to the horizontal plane, its horizontal projection gives the true size of that face; and the vertical projection, the altitude perpendicular to the faces BCEF. Hence the prism is thus fully given by its projections, since a body is said to be completely given, when, as is true in this case, such of its dimensions are known as enable one to find the area of its surface, or its solidity.

Still more clearly is it evident, that, in Fig. 8, the plan, *abcd*, gives the true width and thickness of the prism, and the elevation, the width and height. That is, the two projections, together, give the three dimensions of the prism in their real size.

Thus it will be seen in all the subsequent figures, that the projections of objects give their real forms, as seen when looking perpendicularly towards the planes of projection, and that when these objects are placed in simple positions with respect to those planes, as they always may be, their projections will give the simple dimensions of those objects, as in Fig. 8.

Note.—The figures in this chapter, and others like them, are nothing else than examples of the " military perspective," or cabinet projections, explained in my " Elementary Projection Drawing," Div. IV., Chap. V. They are, therefore, as is evident by examination, *exact constructions*, representative of models of construc tions in space.

CHAPTER III.

THE CONSTRUCTION OF THE PERSPECTIVES OF OBJECTS FROM THEIR PROJECTIONS.

56. The preceding pictorial representatives of models of projections, may suffice to render the subject of projections of given objects intelligible. We therefore proceed to illustrate the remaining points in (37) viz. the projections of the point of sight (29), the visual rays (30), and the constructions of true perspectives of objects from their projections, instead of from the objects themselves (41).

We have seen that the eye is at an indefinitely great distance from each plane of projection, successively, in viewing objects as seen in projection (46). But objects, as seen in perspective, are supposed to be viewed from points at ordinary finite distances.

The point of sight is therefore projected like any other point, as in Fig. 3.

57. Since the perspective of a given point in space, is the point where the visual ray from that given point pierces the perspective plane (35), it is necessary, in the next place, to understand the method of finding the point in which a given line pierces any vertical plane, taken as a perspective plane (36).

For this purpose, see Fig. 9. Here GHII' is the horizontal plane, and GV, the vertical plane. AE is any line in space, joining the point A, behind the vertical plane, with the point E in front of it. Aa and Ee represent the vertical projecting lines which meet the horizontal plane at some points represented by a and e, and which therefore determine ae as the horizontal projection of AE. Likewise the projecting lines Aa' and Ee', which are perpendicular to the vertical plane, give $a'e'$ as the vertical projection of AE.

This being established, we have, by referring particularly to the line AE itself, the following, as the *first method* of explaining the construction of the desired point.

It is evident from the figure, as just described, that any line, as AE, must pierce the vertical plane somewhere in its own vertical projection, $a'e'$. Also, as AE is directly over its own horizontal projection, ae, it must meet the vertical plane in some point directly

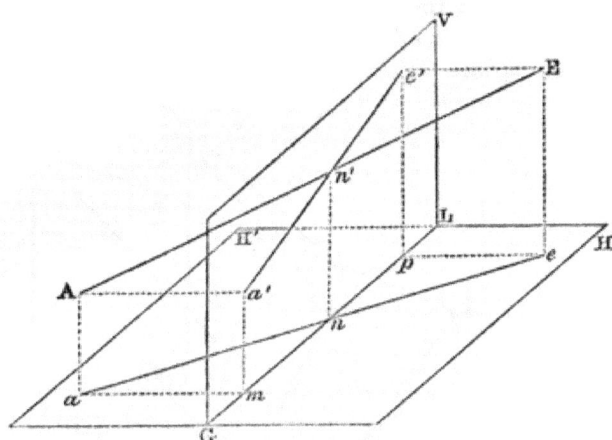

FIG. 9.

over the point *n*, where its horizontal projection meets the vertical plane, in the ground line. Hence AE meets the vertical plane at *n′*, the intersection of *a′e′* with *nn′*, a line perpendicular to the ground line at *n*.

58. Now suppose the line itself, AE, to be removed, leaving only its projections, *ae* and *a′e′*, to be used in finding the point *n′*. In this case, we have the following, as the *second method*—and the usual practical one—of explaining the construction of *n′*. If a point lies in the vertical plane, its vertical projection is the point itself; and its horizontal projection is in the ground line (45). Conversely, if a point in the ground line is the horizontal projection of some point, that point is in the vertical plane. Hence in Fig. 9, *n*, where the horizontal projection, *ae*, of the given line meets the ground line, is the horizontal projection of that point of the line in which it pierces the vertical plane. This point itself being, as already explained, in the vertical projection, *a′e′*, of the given line, and also in a perpendicular to the ground line at *n*, it is at *n′*, the intersection of *nn′* with *a′e′*.

Remarks.—a. The construction of *n′* being of constant occurrence in exact perspective drawings, both of the above explanations should be memorized, as well as clearly understood, until they become thoroughly familiar.

b. It is now evident that if E is the position of the eye, and GLV the perspective plane, AE is a visual ray, and *n′* is the perspective of the point A, as seen by the eye at E.

59. In further illustration of the manner of finding the perspec-

tives of objects from their projections, Fig. 10 is added, which is a
pictorial representation of the construction of the perspective of a
straight line in space.

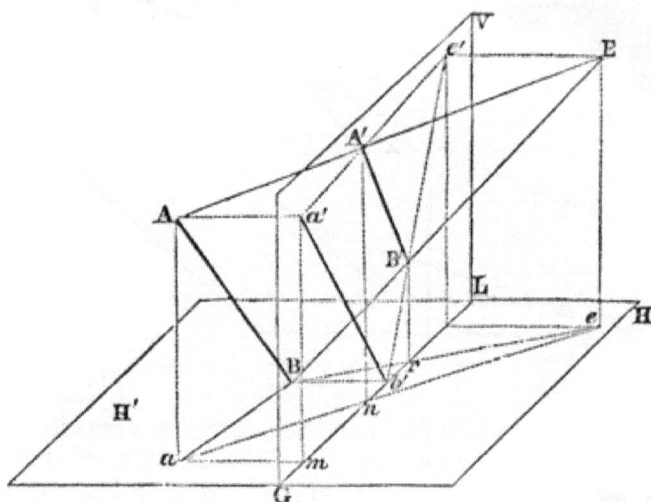

Fig. 10.

GHH' is the horizontal plane. GV, the vertical plane, is, *as
usual*, taken also for the perspective plane. Let AB be any
oblique line, behind the perspective plane, and meeting the horizontal plane at B, and whose perspective is to be found. Let E, in
front of the perspective plane, be the point of sight. By (43) e
and e' are the projections of the point of sight. Likewise, a'
and a' are the projections of A. The point B, being in the horizontal plane, is its own projection on that plane, and by (45) b', in
the ground line, is its vertical projection. Therefore, aB and $a'b'$
are the projections of the given line. Now, AE is the visual ray
from A, the upper end of the line AB; ae and $a'e'$ are the projections of this ray. Then by (58) this ray pierces the perspective
plane at A', which is, therefore, (58b) the perspective of A. Likewise BE is the visual ray from B, the foot of the given line; and
Be and $b'e'$ are its projections. This ray pierces the perspective
plane at B', which is, therefore, the perspective of B. Hence A'B'
is the perspective of AB.

Remarks.—a. Since the perspective, or vertical plane, is placed
between the eye and the given object, the object lies behind the
perspective plane, as in Figs. 8 and 10; hence its plan will appear
behind the ground line.

b. In all cases where two planes of projection are used, as just shown, the vertical plane of projection is also the perspective plane, and, therefore, contains both the vertical projection and the perspective of the given object.

c. By erasing the lines AB, BE, and AE, so as to leave only their projections, also the projecting lines A*a*, A*a'*, B*b'*, E*e*, and E*e'*, the remaining lines would show pictorially the construction of the perspective, A'B', from the projections, only, of AB, and of the ray AE.

The construction of such a figure is left for the student to make.

CHAPTER IV.

REAL PROJECTIONS, AND PERSPECTIVES MADE FROM THEM.

60. All the preceding figures are only the *pictures of projections*, and *pictures of the perspectives*, made from those projections, and *not* the projections and the perspectives themselves. They are pictorial representatives of the models which would show given objects, the eye, the perspective plane, and visual rays, as they actually exist in space.

It is, therefore, next to be found how these projections and perspectives themselves are represented. In doing this, we seek first the method of representing the planes of projection, which are really at right angles to each other, upon a single flat surface, as a sheet of paper.

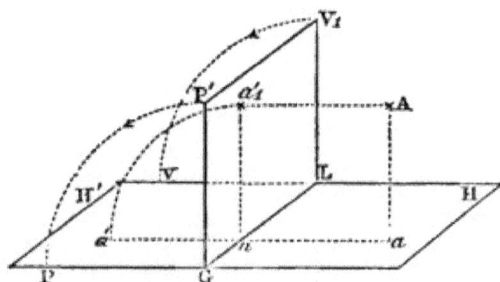

FIG. 11.

61. From Fig. 11 it is evident that, if the vertical plane, GVV₁, be revolved directly back about the ground line, GL, as an axis, until it coincides with the back portion, GII′, of the horizontal plane, all the points of the vertical plane will describe circular arcs in the direction of the arrows, and in planes perpendicular to the ground line. If, then, A be a point in space, and in front of the vertical plane, and a and a', its projections, a', will describe the quadrant $a'_1 a'$, and will be found in the line ana', a perpendicular to the ground line through the horizontal projection, a, of the given point.

62. According, now, to this illustration, the following method

is universally agreed upon as the one to be practically adopted in representing projections.   •

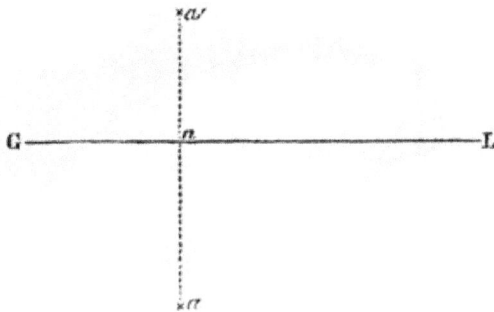

FIG. 12.

Having drawn any line, GL, Fig. 12, upon the drawing paper, to represent the ground line, it is understood that all that portion of the paper below or in front of the ground line, represents the front part of the horizontal plane of projection, and that the portion above or back of the ground line, represents both the back part of the horizontal plane, GII', Fig. 11, and the vertical plane, GV, Fig. 11.

Hence, make na and na', Fig. 12, equal respectively to na and na'_1, or na'_1, on Fig. 11, and a and a' will represent, not the *pictures* of the projections of A, but the projections themselves of that point. Accordingly, as in (44), the point supposed is named by its projections, and we say "the point aa'," meaning the point in space whose projections are a and a', and which is at the height, $a'n$, above the horizontal plane, and distance, an, in front of the vertical plane.

63. Having now shown, pictorially, the manner of representing the projections of points, upon the planes of projection when in their real position (43) and as shown after revolution (61) and the manner of finding the perspective of a point, or a line (58b–59) the way is prepared for the connected review embraced in the three following figures, which show *first:* a pictorial representation of the construction of the perspective of a point, on the perspective plane in its *real* position; *second:* a similar view after the revolution of the perspective plane into the plane of the paper; and *third:* an actual construction of the real perspective of a point.

64. In Fig. 13, E is the position of the eye, e is its horizontal projection, and e' is its vertical projection. $Ce' = Ee$ shows the

height of the eye above the horizontal plane, and C e = E e' shows its distance in front of the vertical plane, LGP, which is also the perspective plane.

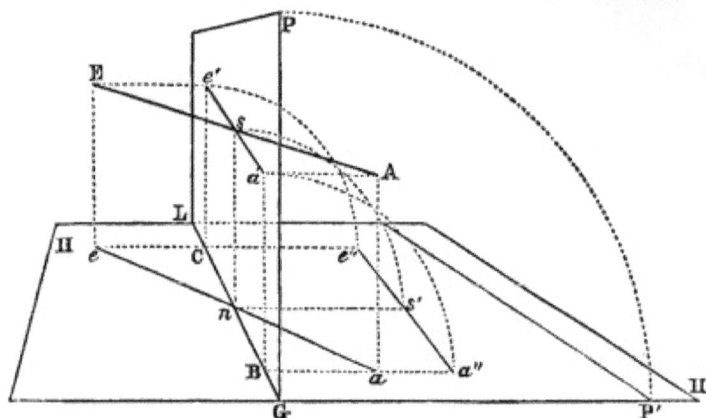

Fig. 13.

A is the point, whose perspective is to be found, a is its horizontal projection, and a' its vertical projection. Ba' = Aa shows the height of A above the horizontal plane GHH; aB = a'A shows its distance behind the perspective plane LGP, and CB shows its distance to the right of the observer standing at e. Thus the position of the point is completely indicated with respect, both to the eye at E, and the perspective plane (22).

We have, now, the following statement of this problem.

> *Given:* GHH,
>   LGP,
>   E, and
>   A.

> *Required,* the perspective of A, given in its projections a and a'; on LGP, as seen from E, given also by its projections e and e'.

> *Construction.* Draw ae and $a'e'$, and note n. At n erect ns perpendicular to GL and note s, where it meets $a'e'$. Then s will be the required perspective of aa', that is, of A (58).

65. This being established, we proceed according to (63) to represent, pictorially, the revolution of the perspective plane backward into the horizontal plane, so as to show the above construction in a single plane, as is done in practice. The several quarter

circles, Fig. 13, represent the revolutions of the several points a', e', etc., about GL as an axis, till they reach the horizontal plane.

Thus LGP' is the revolved position of the perspective plane LGP, and a', s', and e'' are the revolved positions of a', s, and e' respectively. Then a'' e'' is the revolved position of the vertical projection a' e' of the ray AE, and n s' the revolved position of ns, giving s', as the revolved perspective.

Since the horizontal plane is unmoved, all points upon it remain fixed, and a and a'' are the projections of A, e and e'' the projections of E, and ae and $a''e''$ the projections of the visual ray AE.

Observe, now, that when the two planes are no longer shown in their real position, the ray itself, AE, can no longer be shown, so that Fig. 14 shows separately, and pictorially, all of Fig. 13 that can appear when the two planes are represented as one surface. Fig. 14 evidently shows, however, according to the last article, all

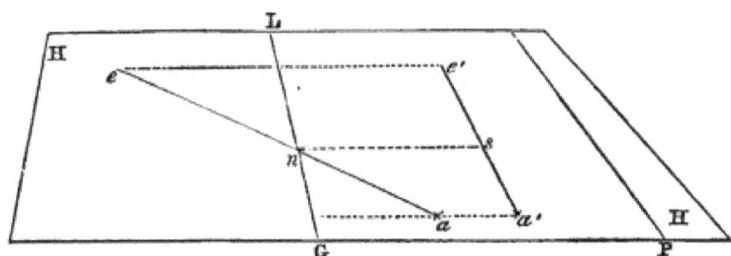

FIG. 14.

that is essential in finding s, the perspective of aa' as seen from the eye at ee'.

67. Finally; Fig. 15 shows the pictorial representation in Fig. 14, transformed into an actual construction, according to (62).

[*Note.*—While a single complete illustration, fully explained, suffices for the purposes of a text book, the learner, in order to avoid confusion of mind in his progress, should make himself perfectly familiar with *each successive stage* of the subject, by constructing a variety of figures, similar to those thus far given.]

Proceeding, now, with Fig. 15, aa' is the given point, at a distance equal to ad, *back* of the vertical plane, and at a distance equal to $a'd$ above the horizontal plane. ee' is the point of sight, at a distance equal to eb *in front* of the vertical plane, and at a distance equal to $e'b$, above the horizontal plane.

From the preceding descriptions, it follows that ae is the horizontal projection of a visual ray from the given point aa', and $a'e'$ is its vertical projection. Then p, the point where the horizontal projection of this ray meets the ground line GL, is the horizontal projection of that point of the ray in which it pierces the vertical,

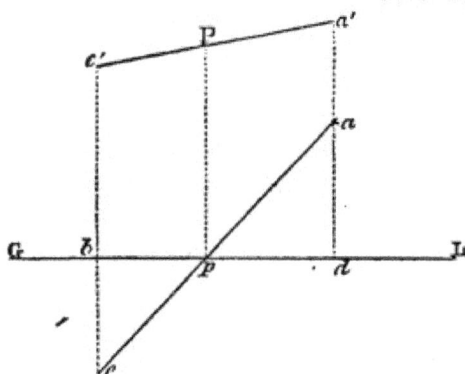

FIG. 15.

i. e. the perspective plane (58). The latter point being also in the vertical projection of the ray (57,58) is at P, the intersection of $a'e'$ with pP, a perpendicular to the ground line at p. Therefore P is the perspective of aa', as seen from the point ee'.

68. In order to find the perspective of any object, we have only to find the perspectives of its separate points, exactly as just described. Hence the following explanations will not be so minute for each point, as the one just given. We shall now proceed to explain the construction of the perspectives of the leading elementary solids, viz. the *prism, pyramid, cylinder, cone*, and *sphere ;* together with various subordinate practical particulars. And though this may not *in itself* interest the learner as much as the representation of objects whose perspectives have more of pictorial effect, yet the recollection that no other method will so concisely afford an equally abundant variety of *universally useful methods of practical operation*, in subsequent practical examples, may suffice to compensate for the comparative inelegance of the perspectives now to be explained.

EXAMPLE 1.—To find the Perspective of a Vertical Square Prism, situated as shown in Fig. 8.

From Fig. 8 it is evident, that when the perspective plane is revolved backward, the lines $c'C'$ and $d'D'$ of the *elevation* (55a) will exactly fall upon the lines cb and da of the plan. Hence, in Fig. 16, ABCD and $c'd'$ C'D' are the correct projections of a square prism standing on the horizontal plane, at the distance $d'D$ behind the vertical or perspective plane.

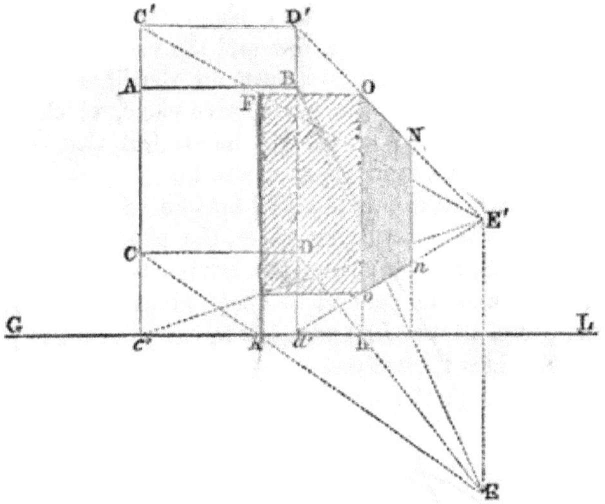

FIG. 16.

Let EE' be the position of the eye. The rays from c' and C', being one directly over the other, have the same horizontal projection, CE. Then by (67) CE — c'E' is the visual ray (58b) from the front left hand corner, Cc', of the base, and f is the perspective of that corner. CE — C'E' is the ray from the corresponding upper corner CC'. It pierces the perspective plane at F, which is therefore the perspective of CC'. Likewise the visual ray DE — d'E' pierces the perspective plane at o, which is therefore the perspective of the point Dd'; and the visual ray DE — D'E' pierces the perspective plane at O, giving the perspective of the point DD'. Hence the figure FfOo is the perspective of CD — $c'd'$ C'D', the front face of the given prism. Finally, BE and d'E' are the projections of the visual ray from the right hand back corner, B, d', of the base of the prism. This ray pierces the perspective plane at n, the perspective of this corner. Also BE—D'E' is the visual ray from the corresponding corner, B,D', of the upper base. This ray gives N as the perspective of B,D'. Then drawing ON, on, and nN, we shall have the complete perspective of the visible edges of the given prism.

69. *Remarks.*—a. Observe that fo and FO are, by the construction, parallel to the ground line GL, and to the lines CD — $c'd'$, and

CD – C'D', of which they are the perspectives. Also that the right hand edges, BD — d' and BD — D', of the bases, are perpendicular to the perspective plane, while their perspectives *on* and ON meet at E', if produced. This is easily explained from elementary geometry. Planes containing the eye and the vertical edges, as at C and D, are vertical planes, standing on the lines CE and DE. Hence they must intersect the perspective plane, which is also vertical, in lines, kF and kO, which will be vertical, that is parallel to the vertical edges of the prism, at C and D.

In like manner, since the top and bottom edges, $c'd'$ and C'D', are parallel to the perspective plane, the planes passed through them and the eye, must intersect the perspective plane, in lines fo and FO, which will be parallel to those given edges. And, generally, the perspectives of all parallels to the perspective plane, are parallel to the lines themselves.

b. Planes through the eye, and the edges DB–d' and DB–D'

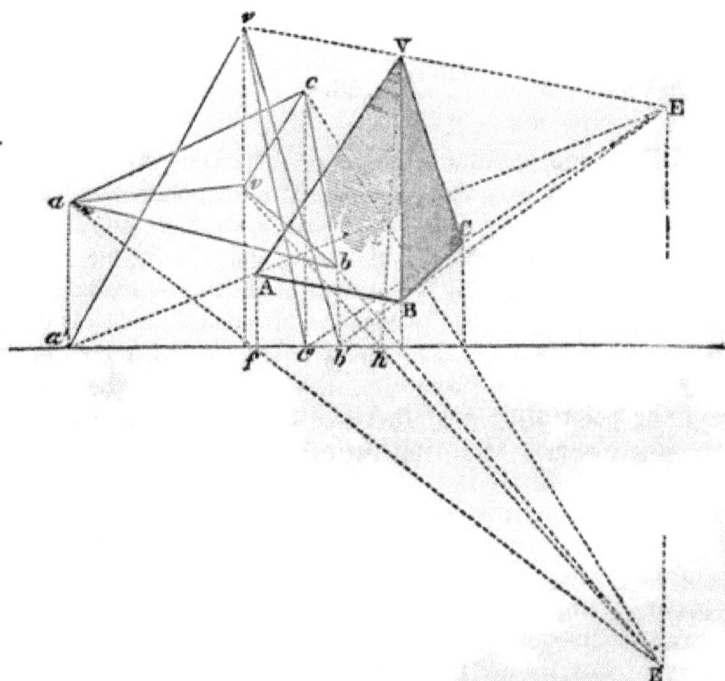

FIG. 17.

which are perpendicular to the perspective plane, will contain the visual rays from D,d' and DD' and will, themselves, be perpendicular to that plane. They will therefore intersect each other in a line, perpendicular to the perspective plane at E′. Hence their intersections with the perspective plane, which will be the indefinite perspectives (37) of the edges contained in them, will be the lines d'E′, and D′E′.

EXAMPLE 2.—**To find the Perspective of a Triangular Pyramid.**

This example embraces the perspectives of oblique lines. $abc - v$ and $a'b'c' - v'$, Fig. 17, are the projections of a triangular pyramid, standing on the horizontal plane, and behind the vertical plane. E and E′ are the projections of the point of sight. aE $- a'$E′ is the visual ray from the point aa' of the base of the pyramid. This ray pierces the perspective plane at A, the intersection of fA and a'E′. A is therefore the perspective of aa'. Likewise, by the rays bE $- b'$E′, and cE $- c'$E′, we find B and C, the perspectives of bb' and cc'. vE $- v'$E′ is the visual ray from the vertex vv', and it pierces the perspective plane at V, the intersection of hV and v'E′, giving V as the perspective of vv'.

Joining the points now found, ABC $-$V is the perspective of the given pyramid $abc - v - a'b'c' - v'$, as seen from EE′.

Remark.—The student should construct other figures by the above method, till quite familiar with it.

CHAPTER V.

REMOVAL OF PRACTICAL DIFFICULTIES ARISING FROM THE CONFU
SION OF PROJECTIONS AND PERSPECTIVES.

§ I. — *First Method.   Translation, forward, of the Perspective
Plane.*

70. The perspective plane being between the eye and the given
object, the plan of that object must lie behind the ground line.
Also, as the perspective plane contains both the vertical projection
and the perspective of the object, these two must both fall upon the
plan, when the perspective plane is revolved back into the horizontal plane ; as seen in the last two examples.

The confusion of lines arising from this source is sufficiently apparent from Figs. 16 and 17, though they embrace very simple
objects, and remove the perspectives as far as possible from the
projections, by placing the eye considerably to one side of the
projections.

71. Hence, before proceeding further with practical constructions,
we shall present a simple method of obviating the difficulty just
mentioned. This method consists in transferring the perspective
plane, with all the points in it, directly forward, far enough to allow
it to be revolved back so as to lodge the figures in it entirely below,
or in front of, the plan.

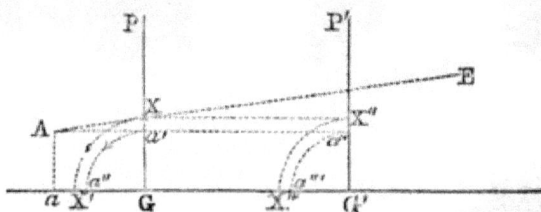

FIG. 18.

This method is illustrated in Fig. 18. A is a point whose projections are *a* and *a'*, on planes seen edgewise and in their real positions at right angles to each other, at *a*GG' and GP. E is the
place of the eye. Then X represents the perspective of *aa'*.

When, now, the perspective plane GP is revolved back as shown by the arrows, carrying a' and X to a'' and X', a,X' and a'' will be crowded together. But suppose the perspective plane to be first moved forward—carrying along the points a' and X—to a new position G'P', and then to be revolved. The perspective, X'', will then appear at X''', free from the plan ; and it may also be freed from the elevation, in practice, by erasing portions of the latter from time to time, as the construction of the perspective progresses, or by transferring only the perspective points.

The elementary examples of the last chapter are here continued, according to the method just explained.

EXAMPLE 3.—**To find the Perspective of a Cube, which stands obliquely with respect to the perspective plane.**

See Fig. 19. $aceg$ is the plan of a cube thus situated, and $a'b'c'f'$ is its elevation.

The ground line GL indicates the first position of the perspective plane, and G'L' shows its position after translation forward. E is the horizontal projection of the point of sight. Being in the horizontal plane, its position is not affected by the translation of the perspective plane. E' is the vertical projection of the point of sight, shown only on the second position of the perspective plane, since it is used only there. For a similar reason, the vertical projections of the visual rays are shown only on the second position of the perspective plane. aE is the horizontal projection of the visual rays from the two points aa' and a,b' (Ex. 1.). By making $b''a''=b'a'$, and in $a'b'$ produced, we find the projections of a' and b' upon the second position of the perspective plane. Likewise we find f'', e'', c'', etc. Then, for example, aE and a''E' are the projections, employed, of the visual ray from a,a''; or, more briefly (58) aE—a''E' is the visual ray from a,a''. This ray pierces the perspective plane at A, the intersection of a''E' with the perpendicular to GL, at h, where the horizontal projection, aE, of the ray meets the *real*, that is the *original* position of the ground line (57-8). Then A is the required perspective of a,a''. Other points as B,F, etc., of the perspective of the cube may be found in a precisely similar manner. The construction of some of the points is therefore omitted, to avoid unnecessary confusion of the figure. Thus, the perspective of the point, c,d'' will be at the intersection of a line d''E' with the perpendicular to GL at n. The perspective of the back upper corner g,g'' is likewise at the intersection of a ray from g'' to E', with the perpendicular to GL at o.

To avoid the acute intersections, as at B, by the method of two planes, without setting E,E' far to one side, as in Fig. 17, translate the points, as a,b'', of the given object, only, to one side in a direction parallel to the ground line, and then find their perspectives, as B' (not shown) which will be well defined. Then a parallel to the ground line, through B', will intersect either b''E', or hB, giving B by a well defined intersection. Observe that E,E' is not moved.

Remark. — The perspectives of other plane-sided objects, in various positions, should be constructed by the learner, by the method just explained. For example, let Fig. 17 be re-constructed according to the method of Fig. 19.

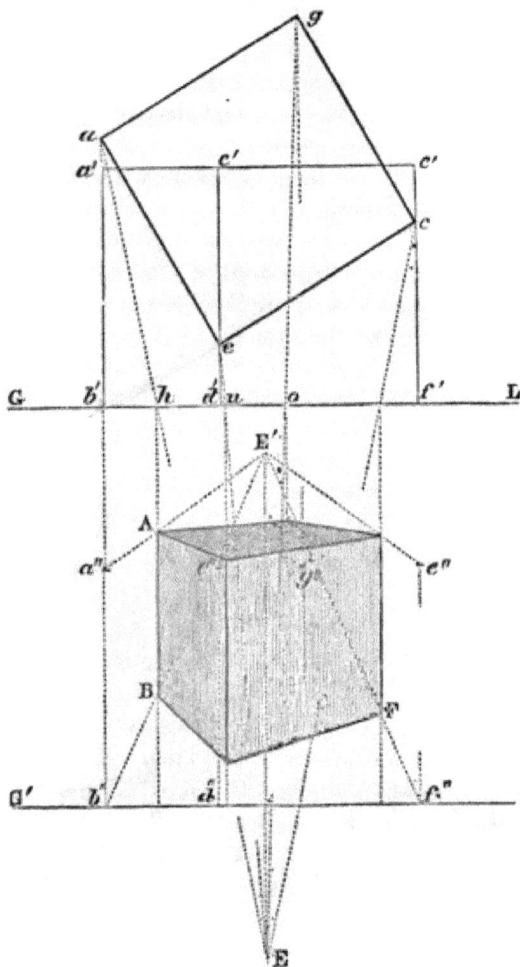

Fig. 19.

§ II. *Second Method. Use of three Planes.*

72. The confusion of the diagrams, arising from the confounding together of the perspective with either or both of the projections

of the given object, may be still further avoided by making the
perspective plane a third plane, separate from both of the planes
of projection, and at right angles to both of them.

This is accomplished in the manner illustrated in Fig. 20.

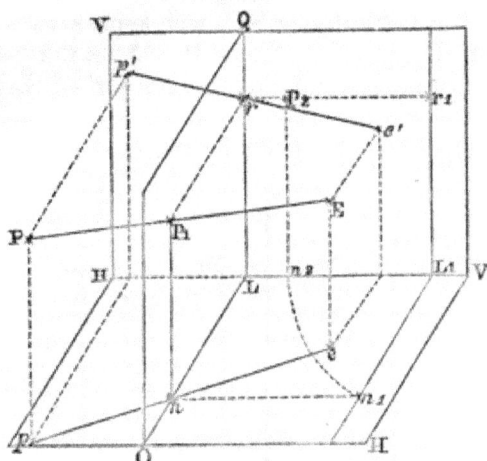

FIG. 20.

OIHH is the horizontal plane of projection; VV, the vertical
plane of projection, and OLQ the perspective plane. P is a point
in space, whose perspective is to be found. p represents its horizontal, and p' its vertical projection. E is the position of the eye,
e its horizontal, and e' its vertical projection. Then PE represents
the visual ray, whose intersection with OLQ will be the perspective of P. pe is the horizontal, and $p' e'$ the vertical projection
of this ray. The perspective plane OLQ is perpendicular to both
of the other given planes, and LQ is its intersection with the vertical plane of projection. LQ is called the trace of OLQ upon the
vertical plane of projection. Then, as in previous cases, P_1, the
perspective of P, is in the line $n P_1$, perpendicular to the ground
line OL at n. Likewise it is obviously in the line $r P_1$, perpendicular to the trace LQ at r. Hence P is at the intersection of $n P_1$
and $r P_1$.

73. Now in order to bring all three of these planes into a single
surface, as is done in practical drawing, the perspective plane may
be revolved about its trace LQ till it coincides with the vertical
plane VV, which may then be revolved back as usual around the
principal ground line, HL_1. But by such a proceeding, the perspective of an object would by revolution fall upon the vertical

projection of that object. Hence the perspective plane is moved
towards the eye, and parallel to its first position to some convenient new position as $n_1L_1r_1$, before being revolved. Then, as
every point of the perspective plane moves parallel to the ground
line, n will appear at n_1, and r at r_1, and after revolution in the direction n_1n_2, the vertical line nP$_1$ will appear at n_2P$_2$, and th
horizontal line rP$_1$, at r_1P$_2$. Hence P will be the perspective of
P, after the translation and first revolution of the perspective
plane.

74. The perspective of a point by the method of three planes,

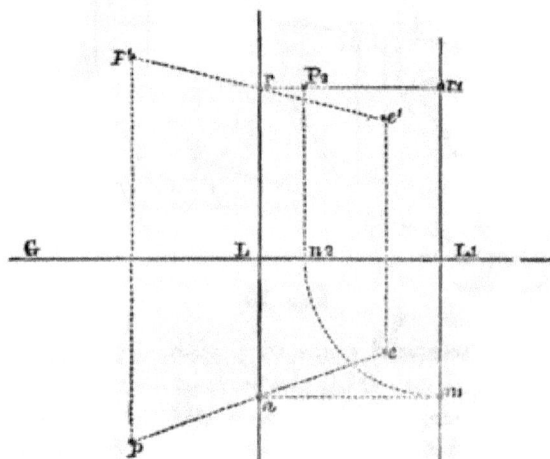

Fig. 21.

shown pictorially in Fig. 20, is shown as an actual construction in
Fig. 21. The former figure is exactly transformed into the latter
by making the corresponding distances equal in both, and by letter-
ing the same points with the same letters, so far as shown at all.

pp' is the given point, given by its projections. ee' is likewise
the point of sight, nLr the first, and $n_1L_1r_1$ the second position of
the perspective plane, thus indicated as at right angles to both
planes of projection. $pe—p'e'$ is the visual ray from pp', which
pierces the perspective plane nLr at a point whose projections are
n and r. After translating this plane, parallel to the ground line,
to the position $n_1L_1r_1$, these points appear at n_1 and r_1. Then, by
revolving the perspective plane from $n_1L_1r_1$ into the vertical plane
of projection, the point n_1r_1 describes a horizontal arc about the
point L_1, r_1 as a centre. The projections of this arc are n_1n_2 and
r_1P , and P$_2$ thus appears as the perspective of pp'.

Remarks.—a. The perspective plane must, in Fig. 21, be translated to the right so as to revolve to the left, in order that the right
hand of the perspective may continue to correspond with the right
hand of the object drawn. This will be obvious on inspection in
the succeeding examples, wherever three planes shall be used.

b. Either of the methods of disposing of the perspective plane,
explained in this chapter, will be used at pleasure in the solutions
which follow. The student is advised to solve the subsequent
problems, on three planes, when two are used by the author, and
vice versa.

To assist therefore in becoming more familiar with the use of
three planes, the following practical problem is given.

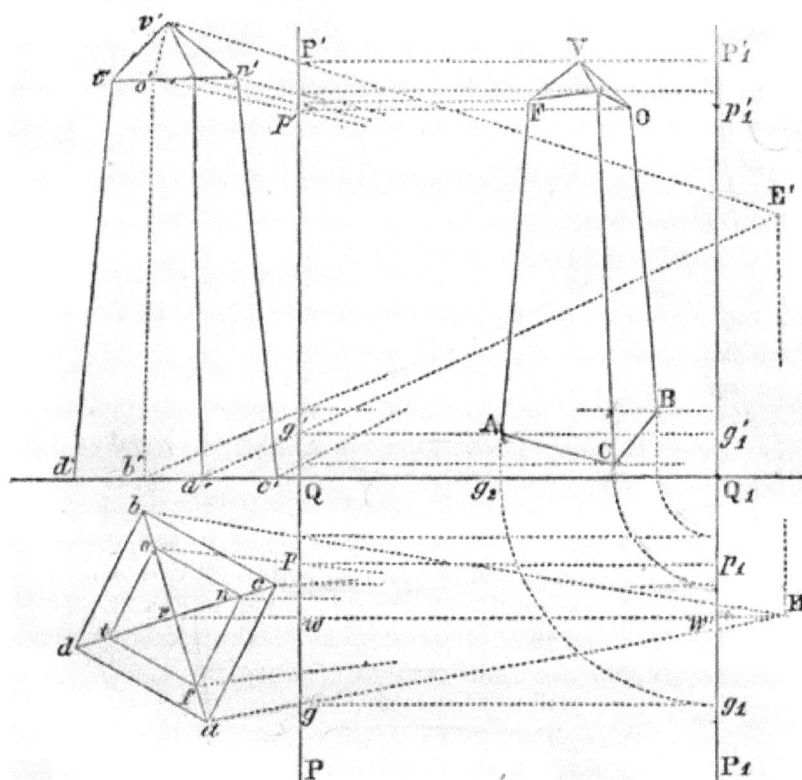

FIG. 22.

EXAMPLE 4.—To find the Perspective of an Obelisk, composed of a frustum of a long pyramid, capped by a short
pyramid.

Let the square $acbd$—$c'd'$, Fig. 22, be the horizontal and vertical projections of the base of the obelisk ; and v–$fnot$—v'–$n't'$ the projections of the cap pyramid.

Let PQP' be the first and *real* position of the perspective plane, at right angles to both planes of projection. Let $P_1Q_1P'_1$, be its second position, parallel to the first, from which it is revolved round P'_1Q_1, its intersection with the vertical plane, until it coincides with that plane. EE' is the point of sight.

To find the perspective of any point, as aa', of the base. aE and a'E' are the projections of the visual ray from this point. This ray pierces the perspective plane at gg'. This point, after translation, appears at g_1g_1', found by drawing gg_1 and $g'g_1'$, parallel to the ground line. After its revolution through the horizontal quarter circle whose projections are g_1g_2 and g_1 A, it appears at A, the intersection of g_1'A with g_2A, perpendicular to the ground line QQ_1.

In like manner C and B, the perspectives of cc' and bb' are found.

Note that bb', the invisible corner of the base as seen in vertical projection, is the right hand corner, to the eye at EE' looking in the direction Ev.

To find the perspective of any point of the cap pyramid, we also proceed just as before. Thus, oE—o'E' is the visual ray from the corner oo'. This ray pierces the perspective plane PQP' at pp', which is translated to p_1p_1', and from that position revolved in a horizontal arc, as before, to O, the perspective of oo'.

Remarks.—*a.* Every point of the perspective being thus found in precisely the same manner, the construction of several of them is left to be made by the student.

b. Observe also, that as the operations in Figs. 21 and 22 are precisely similar, the perspective of any object, by the method of three planes, is simply, and only, a continued repetition of the construction of the perspective of a single point, as in Fig. 21.

c. Practice is required, however, to enable the learner to understand readily the *form and position of any given object from its projections,* and to determine easily, by mere inspection, *the projections of those points which are seen from the given point of sight.* Hence, again, the student is advised to construct the perspectives of various other simple objects, from their projections, as in this example.

CHAPTER VI.

PROJECTIONS AND PERSPECTIVES OF CIRCLES, AND OF BODIES HAVING
PARTLY OR WHOLLY CIRCULAR BOUNDARIES.

75. The outlines of almost all artificial objects will be found, by analyzing them, to consist of straight lines and circular lines. Having now shown how to find the perspectives of points, straight lines, and plane sided figures, both pictorially and by actual construction, we next proceed to explain the construction of the perspectives of circles, and of various bodies bounded in part, at least, by circles.

EXAMPLE 5.—**To find the Perspective of a Circle lying in the horizontal plane**.

The method by two planes, with the vertical or perspective plane translated forward before being revolved back into the horizontal plane (71) is here employed. See Fig. 23.

Let *acde* be the horizontal projection of the given circle. As this circle lies in the horizontal plane, its vertical projection, *a'd'*, must lie in the ground line LL (45). Now let the perspective plane, which is perpendicular to the paper at LL, be translated forward to the parallel position L'L', and then, as usual, revolved backwards into the horizontal plane, or plane of the paper. Then take EE' as the point of sight, and let all the vertical projections be shown on the translated position of the perspective plane. Accordingly, *a″d″* will be the new vertical projection of the given circle. *b*E is the horizontal, and *f″*E' the vertical projection of the visual ray from the point *b,f″* in the circle. The point *n*, where the horizontal projection *b*E meets the ground line, LL, is the horizontal projection of that point of the ray itself in which it pierces the perspective plane (58). The latter point is at once in the perpendicular, *n*B, to the ground line, and in the vertical projection *f″*E' of the same ray. Hence the desired point is B, which is the perspective of *b*, *f″*.

[This being a new form of example, the construction of the perspective of one point is explained as minutely as if it had not been

fully explained already. The details of the explanation will there
fore be omitted in future similar constructions.]

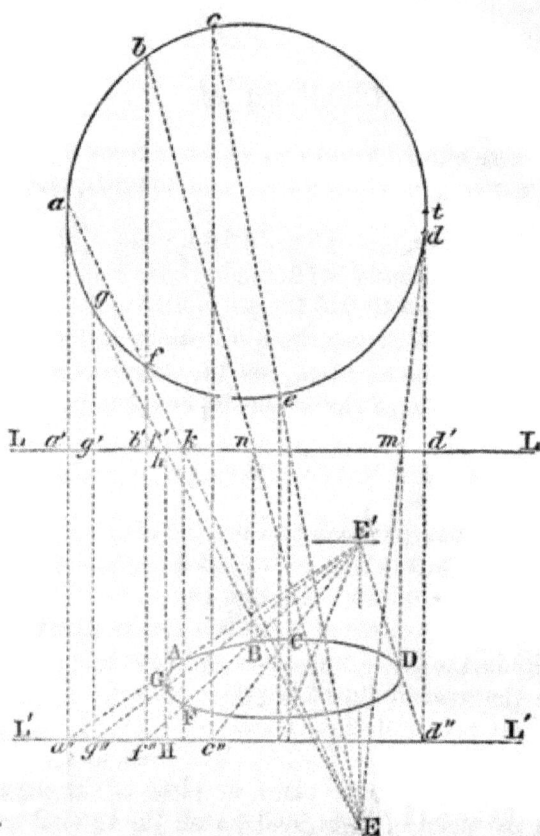

FIG. 23.

The ray cE–$c'E'$ pierces the perspective plane at C, which is
therefore the perspective of c,c''. In like manner the perspectives
of any other points can be found.

By inspection of the vertical projection, $a''d''$, it appears that
the extreme visual rays, as $a''E'$, as seen in vertical projection, are
those which proceed from the opposite ends of the diameter whose
horizontal projection is at. Hence rays from points, as g, before
that diameter, or b, behind it, find their vertical projections, $g''E'$
and $f''E'$ within $a''E'$. Hence no point of the perspective of the

circle can appear outside of the ray $a''E'$, and therefore the perspective must be tangent to $a''E'$, at A, the perspective of aa'.

The similar result, at the perspective of t, is not shown, as it could not appear distinctly on account of the position of EE'.

The rays whose horizontal projections are tangent to the plan at g and d, include the other rays between them. Hence all points of the perspective are between the perpendiculars mD and hG, and the perspective is tangent to these perpendiculars at D and G.

The perspectives of tangents, parallel to the ground line, will be tangents to the perspective and parallel to L'L'. Having now six tangents with their points of contact, besides other points, the perspective curve can be very accurately sketched.

76. In the previous perspectives of plane-sided figures, which are distinguished by well defined edges and corners, however viewed, it will be observed that it can be determined, by simple inspection, which edges will be visible from the point of sight. But, in the case of objects bounded partly or wholly by continuous curved surfaces, the consequent partial or total absence of limiting edges makes it necessary to discover the visible boundaries by more or less of preliminary construction. Hence, a few additional definitions and principles are introduced here for use in the following problems:

77. Other planes than the planes of projection, go by the general name of *auxiliary planes*.

Their positions are indicated by their intersections with the planes of projections, called their *traces*.

Each of these traces takes its name from the plane of projection in which it is found.

78. The point where either trace meets the ground line is where the plane cuts the ground line; hence *both traces of a plane must meet the ground line at the same point*, if they meet it at all.

The traces of a plane will meet the ground line unless the plane is parallel to that line.

79. If, as in Fig. 24, a plane is vertical, but oblique to the vertical plane of projection, its vertical trace, V T, will be perpendicular to the ground line, G L.

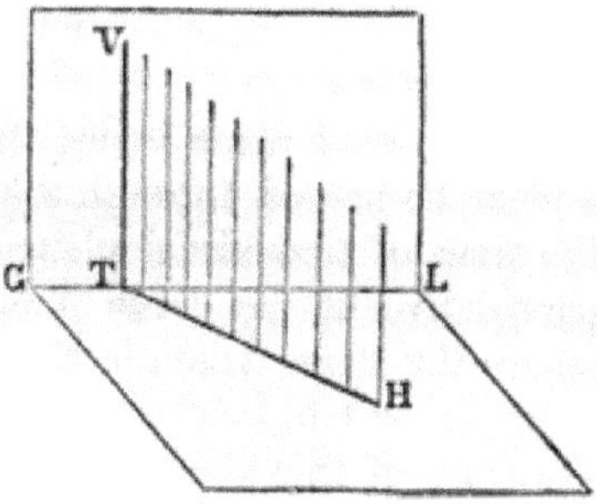

Fig. 24.

80. If, as in Fig. 25, a plane is perpendicular to the vertical

plane of projection, its horizontal trace, H T, will be perpendicular to the ground line, G L.

If a plane is perpendicular to both of the planes of projection, both of its traces will be perpendicular to the ground line, as we have seen in (72–74).

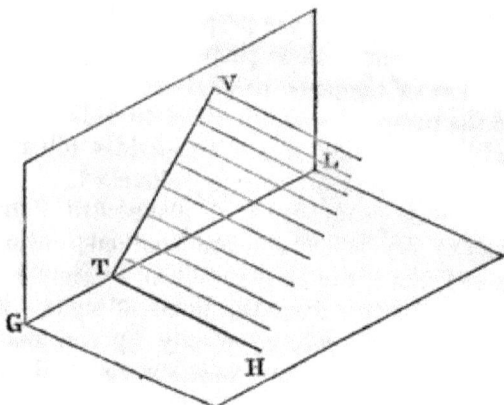

FIG. 25.

81. Again; when a plane is vertical, that is, perpendicular to the horizontal plane, all points and lines in it are horizontally pro-. jected in its horizontal trace; since the horizontal projections of points and lines are vertically under the points and lines themselves.

Likewise, when a plane is perpendicular to the vertical plane of projection, all points and lines in it find their vertical projections in its vertical trace.

82. Any plane containing the point of sight, contains an indefinite number of visual rays, whose directions radiate in all directions, in that plane, and from the eye. Hence such a plane is called a *visual plane.*

83. A visual plane being thus composed of visual rays, if such a plane be passed through a line whose perspective is to be found, the trace of that visual plane on the perspective plane will be the perspective of the given line. See Ex. 1, Rem. *b*, also Fig. 10, where the plane triangle EAB serves to mark the visual plane of indefinite extent, and containing the line AB. A B, is a portion of the trace of this plane on the perspective plane, and is, therefore, the perspective of AB.

84. For the reason just given (82), the point or line at which a visual plane is tangent to a curved surface, is a point or line of the

visible contour of that surface. The perspective of this visible contour or boundary, is the boundary of the required perspective. (32.)

Ex. 6.—To find the Perspective of a Cylinder, standing on the horizontal plane. A cylinder, seen from above, as it stands on the horizontal plane, appears only as a circle. As seen looking forward at it, perpendicularly to the vertical plane, its diameter and height are visible. Hence the circle *afm*, Fig. 26, and the rectangle *n'o'p'r'* are the projections of a cylinder in the given position.

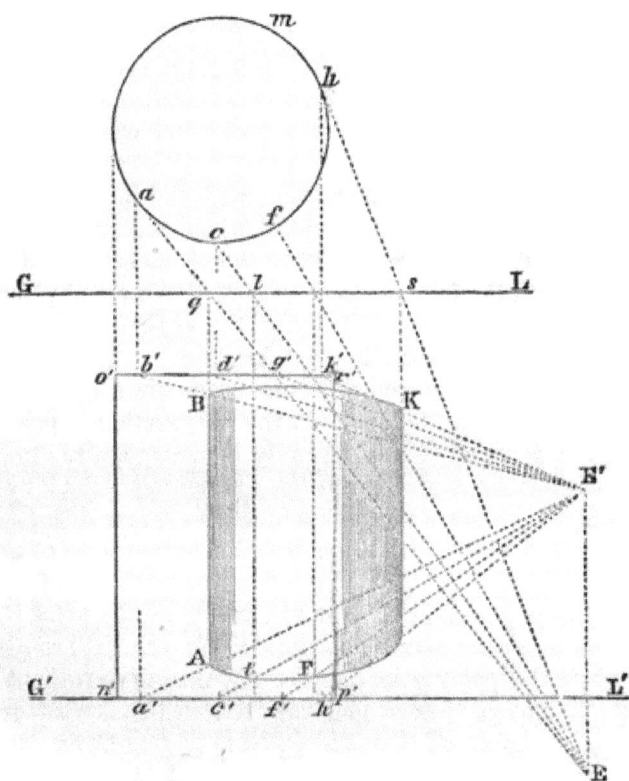

FIG. 26.

This being established, E*h*, tangent to the horizontal projection of the cylinder, is the horizontal trace of a *vertical visual plane*, *tangent to the cylinder along a vertical line of its convex surface at* *h.* Likewise, E*a* is the horizontal trace of a similar plane, tangent to the cylinder along a vertical line at *a*. The vertical projections of these lines are *h'k'* and *a'b'*, and they are the projections of the visible boundaries of the convex surface, as seen from EE'. The tangent planes being vertical, their horizontal traces, as E*h*, are the horizontal projections of both of the visual rays, as E*h*-E'*h'* and E*h*-E'*k'*, from the lower and upper extremities of the lines of con tact, as *h*-*h'k'*. (81.)

This being understood, nothing peculiar remains in the con struction of the perspective, ABFK, of the cylinder. Thus, the perspective of the point *aa'* of the lower base, is found by drawing the visual ray, *a*E-*a'*E', which pierces the perspective plane at A, the intersection of *a'*E' and *q*A, perpendicular to GL at *q*. Like wise, K, the perspective of the point *h*, *k'* of the upper base, is at the intersection of *k'*E' and *s*K, *k'*E' being the vertical projection of the visual ray from *h*, *k'*, and *s*K the perpendicular to GL from the intersection of GL with *h*E, the horizontal projection of the same ray.

The perspective bases are tangent, as at A and B, to the extreme visible elements, as AB; for the visual *plane* containing such extreme element, as *a*—*a'b'* is tangent to the visual *cone* from either base. Therefore, the intersections, as AB, of the visual plane, and A*t*F, or BK, of the visual cone, with the perspective plane are tangent to each other, as at A. (See Art. 85.)

Remarks.—a. Since there will, even when great care is taken, often be slight instrumental errors in the construction of points, the curves in the perspective can be more advantageously drawn by carefully connecting a *few carefully constructed* points by easy curves, than by finding many points in those curves.

b. The figures in this book being designed for purposes of instruction, necessarily show the lines of construction much more fully than is necessary in practice. For example, in finding the point B, Fig. 26, it is not necessary actually to draw either *a*E, *b'*E', or *q*B, but only to mark the point *q* in the line *a*E, then to draw little fragments of *b'*E' and *q*B, just at their intersection B.

Likewise in Fig. 22, all that is essential in finding O, for example, after drawing *o*E—*o'*E', is to make *p*₁'O equal to Q*p*, and in the horizontal line *p'p*₁'.

c. Another matter of still greater practical importance, is the *order* in which the lines of construction should be drawn. *All the lines necessary for finding the perspective of one point, should be drawn, before proceeding to draw those by which a new point is found.* Thus in Fig. 26, draw *a*E, *a*'E', and *q*A, which give the point A. That step being finished, proceed to draw *c*E—*c*'E' and *lt* which determine *t ;* &c.

If, on the other hand, all the lines to E', for example, be drawn before drawing any to E, there will be a considerable liability to mistake in noting wrong intersections; which could not possibly happen by the first method of operating.

d. In every case like this, where points of the vertical projection are shown only on the *second* position of the perspective plane, its *first* position, at GL, need not be supposed to be revolved back into the horizontal plane, but to remain perpendicular to the paper till after translation to its second position at G'L'.

85. The convex surface of a cone, as V–ATB, Fig. 27, is composed of straight lines, which meet at its vertex, V. Hence a plane may be made to rest on this convex surface, along any one of its straight lines. This plane will be tangent to the convex surface.

When this plane contains the point of sight from which the cone is viewed, it will be a *visual* tangent plane, and the line on the cone along which it is tangent, will be a boundary between the visible and invisible portions of the convex surface of the cone. There will evidently be two such tangent visual planes, and boundaries, for any cone.

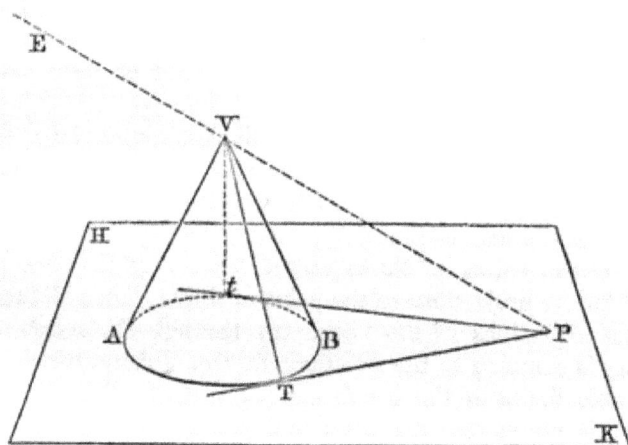

Fig. 27.

In Fig. 27, let E be the point of sight from which the cone V–ATB is seen. Then, as all the lines of the convex surface meet at the vertex, V, the two tangent visual planes through E, will also pass through V, and hence both will contain the visual ray EV through the vertex.

Now let HK be a horizontal plane on which the cone V–ATB stands, and let P be the point where the visual ray EV pierces this plane.

It will then be evident on inspection of this figure, or of a paper model such as the student can make; 1°: That as EP is a line common to both of the tangent planes, P, where EP meets the plane HK, will be a point common to the traces (77) of both of the tangent planes upon the plane HK. 2°: That these traces, being the intersections of planes with each other, will be straight lines; and 3°: That as each visual plane is tangent to the cone along a straight line of its convex surface, the trace of either visual plane upon HK will be tangent to the base of the cone, which lies in the plane HK.

Therefore to find T, and hence TV, a line of contact of a tangent visual plane with the cone, draw PT, tangent to the cone's base, and TV will be the cone's apparent contour on one side, as seen from E. Likewise draw P*t*, and *t*V will be the opposite visible boundary of the cone's convex surface, seen from E.

We will now proceed to show this pictorial illustration in true projection, with the perspective of the cone.

EXAMPLE 7.—**To find the Perspective of a Cone, standing on the horizontal plane.**

1.°—*Preliminary explanation of the projections.* Fig. 28. Three planes are here used, the horizontal and vertical planes of projection; and the perspective plane, placed at right angles to both of them.

The cone is supposed to stand on the horizontal plane. In this position, its horizontal projection is a circle V–TAB, and its vertical projection is an isosceles triangle V′A′B′, whose base equals the diameter of the base of the cone.

2°.—*Construction of the apparent contour of the cone.* Let E and E′ be the projections of the point of sight. Then VE and V′E′ are the projections of the visual ray through the cone's vertex. This ray is common to the two tangent visual planes which contain the visible limits of the cone's convex surface. Now to find N, where this ray pierces the horizontal plane. If a point is in the horizontal plane its vertical projection will be in the ground line, hence, conversely, that point, as N′, of the vertical projection of a line, which is in the ground line, is the vertical projection of that point, as N, which is in the horizontal plane (45). Hence the ray VE–V′E′ pierces the horizontal plane at N, and by (85) NT and N*t* are

the horizontal traces of tangent visual planes, and TV–T′V′ and
tV–t′V′ are their elements of contact with the given cone. These

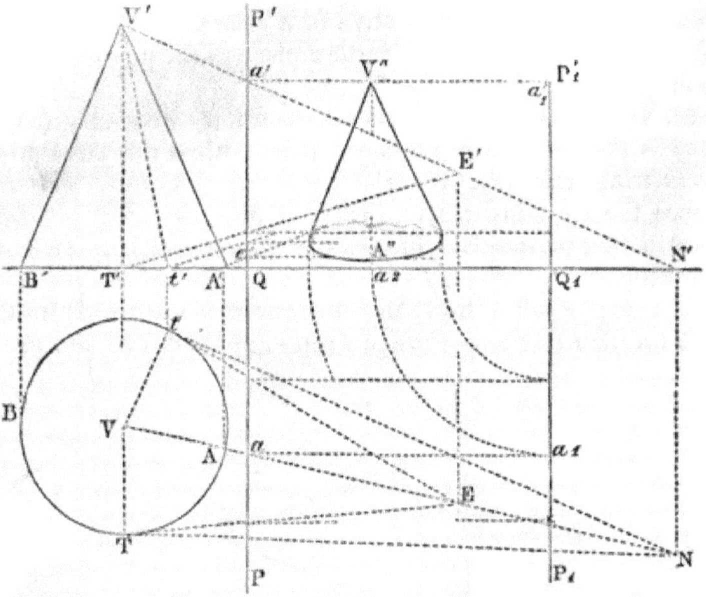

FIG. 28.

elements, with the portion TAt of the base, form the cone's apparent contour.

3°.—*Now to find the perspective of this contour*, that is, of the
cone. The preceding topics (1° and 2°) contain all that is peculiar to
this problem. The construction of the perspective is the same as in
previous examples where three planes were used. The construction of V″, only, is therefore explained to assist in the outset of the
solution, and the rest of the figure is left to be traced out by the
student. The visual ray, VE–V′E′, pierces the perspective plane
in its real position, PQP′, at aa′. After translating this plane to
the right, to any convenient distance, as at P₁Q₁P₁′, it is revolved
about its vertical trace Q₁P₁′, as an axis, and into the vertical plane.
Thus aa′ proceeds to a₁a₁′ and then revolves in the arc a₁a₂–a₁′V″
to V″, the perspective of VV′. (74.)

By constructing, in the same way, the perspectives of TT′ ; AA′,
the point of the base which is nearest to the eye ; and tt′, the perspective figure can be completed.

Remark.—The eye being here placed below the vertex, N and E
fall on the same side of the cone, less than half of which is therefore

visible. When, as in Fig. 27, the eye is above the vertex, P (corre-sponding to N in Fig. 28) and E, are on opposite sides of the vertex, and evidently more than half of the cone will be visible. Let the student construct the perspective of a cone under the latter condi-tion, as above, or taking the vertical plane as the perspective plane, as in Fig. 26.

86. Of the five chief solids of elementary geometry (68), the cone is the one which embraces in its outline the three primary geometrical elements, viz. the *point, straight line,* and *circle.* Hence the most instructive variety of operations will be found in constructing perspectives of cones in various positions, such as the following.

EXAMPLE 8.—**To find the Perspective of a right Cone with a circular base, whose axis is parallel to the ground line.**

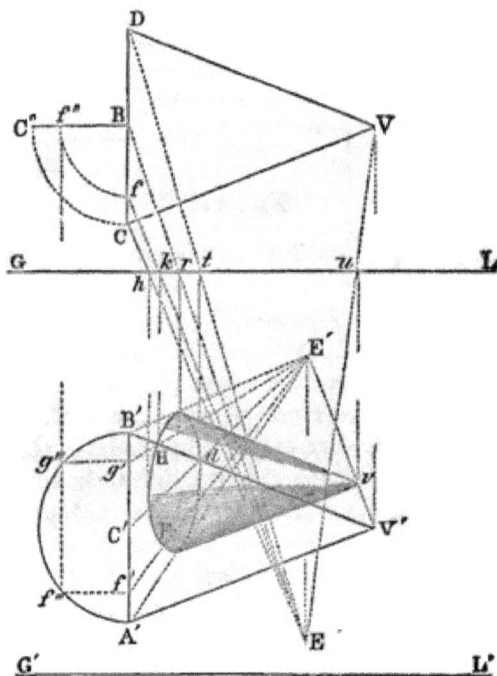

FIG. 29.

We shall employ two planes, and will first explain the projections of the cone. Let GL, Fig. 29, be the first, and G'L' the second position of 'the perspective plane, and let the vertical projection be shown on this second position only.

When the axis of a cone, of the kind here given, is parallel to the ground line, it is parallel to both planes of projection, and the projections of the cone will be simply two equal isosceles triangles, with their bases perpendicular to the ground line. Thus VCD is the horizontal projection of the given cone, and V'A'B' is its vertical projection.

According to (44) A' is the lowest, and B' the highest point on the cone's base. In looking down on a cone, these points will appear, one directly under the other and in the middle of the width of the cone. Hence on the plan, VCD, the point B is the horizontal projection of both A' and B'.

In like manner (44) C is the foremost and D the hindmost point on the cone's base, and C', the middle point of the height of that base, is the vertical projection of both of these points.

To find the projections of any other point in the base. Assume f as the horizontal projection of two such points, since a vertical chord will contain two points, one over the other, of a vertical circle, and two such points will appear in plan as one point. The vertical projection f', of f, cannot be immediately found, since the line from f to f' coincides with A'B' and hence finds nothing to intersect at f', which must therefore be found in some other way; for *it is a law of all constructions in drawing, that a point is always found as the intersection of two known lines.*

Accordingly, revolve the front semicircle, BC, of the base to the position BC'', parallel to the vertical plane. The points f will then appear at f''. The vertical projection of the semicircle after revolution, is the semicircle B'f'''A', and the points f'' will be vertically projected at f''' and g'''. By revolving the semicircle back to its true position, remembering that the axis of revolution is the vertical diameter B-B'A', the points $f''f'''$ and f'' g''' will revolve back n the horizontal arcs whose projections are $f''f$-$f'''f'$ and $f''f$-$g'''g'$, giving g' and f' as the desired vertical projections of the points whose plan is f.

The projections of the cone being now fully explained, nothing peculiar to this problem remains; the construction of the perspective being the same familiar operation already often repeated. Thus, EE' being the point of sight, VE–V'E' is the visual ray through the vertex which by (58) pierces the perspective plane at v, which is therefore the perspective of VV'. Ef is the horizontal projection of both of the rays whose vertical projections are g'E' and f'E'

These rays pierce the perspective plane at H and F, the perspectives of f,g' and ff'. Finding other points of the base in like manner, and joining them, will give the perspective of the base. The perspective of the convex surface of the cone consists merely of two lines from v, tangent to FHd, the perspective of the base.

Remarks.—a. The construction of the perspective of the base i the same that would be used in finding the perspective of any *verti cal* circle which should be also perpendicular to the vertical plane.

b. The same construction of f' and g' would be required in th use of three planes of projection. The perspective of such a circle by the method of three planes is left as an exercise for the student.

EXAMPLE 9.—**To find the Perspective of a Cone, whose axis is parallel to the vertical plane only.**

All that is peculiar to this, and the following example, being the construction of the projections of the cone, they only will be explained; leaving the construction of the perspectives as an exercise for the student.

By (52) it is evident that VO and V'C', Fig. 30, may be taken as the projections of the axis of a cone having the given position, VO being parallel to the ground line GL. The axis being parallel to the vertical plane, the base of the cone will be perpendicular to the same plane and A'B', perpendicular to V'C', and bisected at C', will be its vertical projection.

Four points of the horizontal projection of this base are readily found. A' and B', the highest and lowest points, are horizontally projected at A and B, on the line ABV, which is the common horizontal projection of the axis, and of that diameter of the base, which is parallel to the vertical plane. C', the vertical projection of the foremost and hindmost points, is horizontally projected at C and D; by making OC = OD = A'C'.

A circle, seen obliquely, appears as an ellipse. Accordingly an ellipse, or a smooth oval curve representing one, may now be traced through the points A,C,B, and D, by the aid of an irregular curve (9). Four intermediate points may however be easily found, which if *accurately located* and *regularly distributed*, will render it very easy to trace the required ellipse by hand. For this purpose, we therefore assume o' and n', equidistant from C'. Each of these is the vertical projection of two points of the base. Revolve this base about A'B', till it becomes parallel to the vertical plane, and o' and n' will appear at o'' and n''. $o'o''$ or $n'n''$—perpendicular to A'B'— will then be the true distance of the points at o' and n' before and behind the diameter A'B'. Hence from o' and n' draw projecting lines perpendicular to GL, making $Os = Ot$, and make $sp = sn = tr = to = o'o'' = n'n''$. Then o, n, r, and p will be four regularly distributed points through which, and the four previously found, the elliptical horizontal projection of the cone's base can easily be sketched by hand.

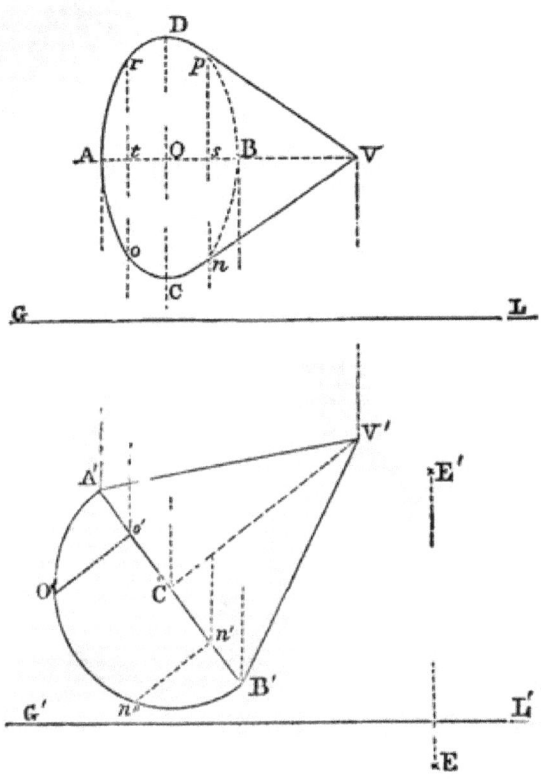

FIG. 30.

To complete the horizontal projection of the cone, merely draw the tangents from V to the ellipse just drawn. The arc pBn between these tangents, is invisible, being on the under side of the cone.

Having now the complete projections of the cone, and the point of sight EE', the perspective can be found as in the previous problems.

EXAMPLE 10.—To find the **Perspective of a Cone,** whose axis is oblique to both planes of projection.

For further variety, the perspective plane is here taken (Fig. 31) as a third plane, PLP', perpendicular to the two principal planes of

projection. It is, however, recommended to the student to solve
this problem with two planes only, besides the auxiliary plane
whose ground line is *gl* ; also to solve the two preceding problems
on three planes.

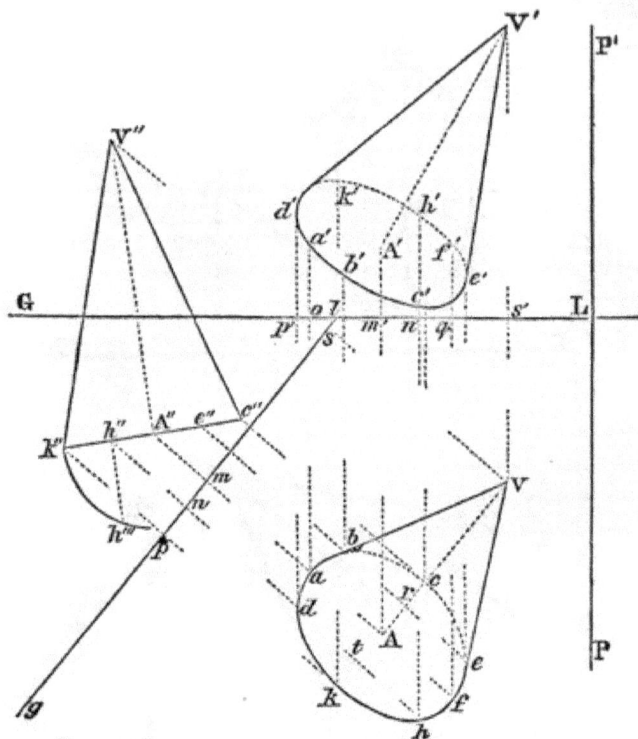

FIG. 31.

Let GL be the principal ground line, and VA and V'A' the projections of the axis of the cone. This axis being oblique to both
planes of projection, the base which is perpendicular to it, is oblique
to them both, also, and hence will appear as an ellipse, in both of
the required projections, so that neither of these projections will
show its real size.

In all the simpler preceding figures, we have seen that at least
one of the two projections shows two of the three dimensions of a
solid in their real size ; so here, where neither of the required
projections possesses this property, we must begin, *as always*, with a
projection upon an auxiliary plane so situated as to show upon it
the real size of two of the dimensions of the cone.

Accordingly gl, parallel to AV, is taken as the ground line of an auxiliary *vertical* plane, parallel to the cone's axis; for two dimensions will appear in full size on such a plane.

Now any number of different vertical projections of one fixed point, will be at equal heights above the ground lines of their respective vertical planes (44), and the two projections of the sam point are always in the same perpendicular to the ground line (61) Hence make $sV'' = s'V'$ and in the line VV'' perpendicular to gl Then make AA'' perpendicular to gl, and $mA'' = m'A'$, and $V''A$ will be the real size of the cone's axis, projected on the auxiliary plane parallel to it.

Next make $c''k''$ perpendicular to $V''A''$ and make $A''c'' = A''k''$; and draw $V''c''$ and $V''k''$, and $V''c''k''$ will be an auxiliary projection of the cone, showing the true size of its altitude $V''A''$ and diameter $c''k''$.

From this auxiliary projection, make the horizontal projection as in the last problem; $Aa = Af = A''c''$; also $br = re = td = th$ equal to $h''h'''$, and projected down from e'' and h''.

Having thus completed two projections, the base in the required vertical projection is found as V' was. Thus $d'p' = h'n' = h'n$; $a'o = f'q' = A'm$, &c. Then sketching the ellipse $a'h'e'c'$, and drawing the tangents to it from V', the required projections of the cone will be complete.

The student can now proceed, as in previous problems where three principal planes at right angles to each other are used, to find the perspective of this cone AV—$A'V'$ on a perspective plane, as PLP', at right angles to both of the principal planes of projection.

Remark.—The operations of projection applied to the bases of the cones in the several preceding problems, are the same that would be necessary in finding the perspectives of isolated circles in similar positions. Hence separate problems upon circles have not been given.

87. Here leaving Cylinders and Cones, whose surfaces are called single curved surfaces, because straight lines can be drawn in certain directions upon them, we pass on to bodies having surfaces called double curved, such as a Sphere, on which no straight line can be drawn.*

---

* As most double curved surfaces in the arts are found on small objects, urns vases, &c., which may be drawn by the eye after their larger supporting or surround

EXAMPLE 11.—To find the Perspective of a Sphere.

88. This example is first taken, since a sphere is the simplest pos
sible double curved surface, inasmuch as the section of it made by
any plane, is a circle.

From the fact just stated, it might at first be supposed that the
perspective of a sphere would always *be* a circle ; but not so, though
it would always *appear* (39) as a circle, from the given point of
sight. For the visual rays from the apparent contour of a sphere
will always form a cone, with a circular base which is this same contour. But the intersection of this cone with the perspective plane,
which will be the perspective of the sphere, will not be a circle
unless the perspective plane is perpendicular to the axis of this cone,
that is to the visual ray from the centre of the sphere. This
statement touches on the subject of conic sections, but the student
can easily satisfy himself of its truth by placing a paper cone
around a ball, observing its circle of contact with the sphere, supposing its vertex to be the place of the eye, and then intersecting
the cone between its vertex and the sphere by planes in various
positions.

There are two quite different methods of determining the apparent contour, whose perspective constitutes the perspective of the
sphere. The determination of this apparent contour forms the chief
portion of the solution of the problem, and to it we therefore first
particularly attend.

For further and instructive variety, we will represent one of these
methods of finding the apparent contour on two planes; and the
other on three planes.

First Method.*—The projections of a sphere will evidently be
two equal circles, whose centres will be in the same perpendicular
to the ground line. Then, in Fig. 32, let the circle with O for its
centre be the horizontal projection of a sphere, whose centre is at a
distance behind the perspective plane equal to the distance of O
from the ground line LL. The equal circle whose centre is O', i
he vertical projection of the same sphere, and the height of O
above LL is the height of the centre of the sphere above the horizontal plane. E and E' are the projections of the point of sight,
and the vertical plane is taken also as the perspective plane.

---

ing objects shall have been found, the two following problems may be omitted at the
discretion of the teacher.

  * This method being chiefly valuable as an intellectual exercise in the conception
of positions and motions in space, it may be omitted at the discretion of the teacher

It is now evident that, if a vertical visual plane EO*b* be drawn through the centre of the sphere, it will cut a vertical great circle

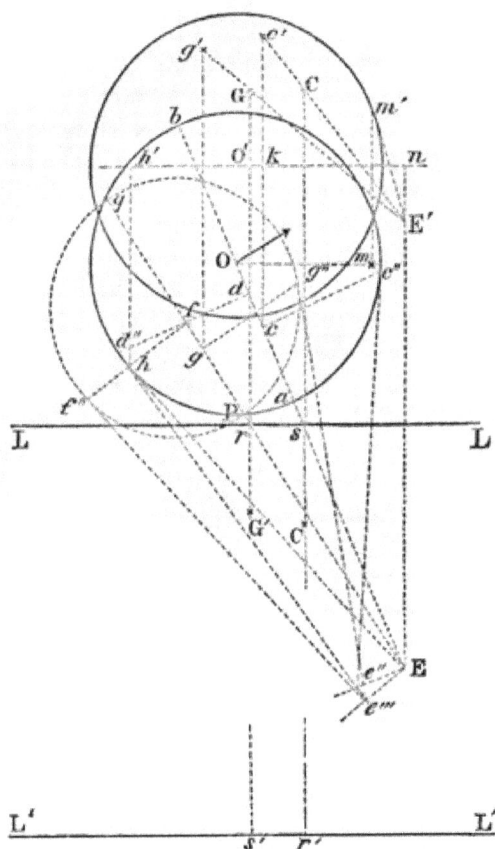

FIG. 32.

from the sphere, to which two tangent visual rays may be drawn. The points of tangency of these visual rays will, as such, be points of the apparent contour of the sphere. But to show these rays, the plane EO*b* must be revolved to a position parallel to one of the planes of projection. Let it be revolved about the horizontal diameter, *ab*, of the sphere, till it becomes parallel to the horizontal plane of projection. The vertical great circle will evidently then appear in the great circle *hc'b*, on *ab* as a diameter. The eye is at the vertical distance E'*n* below the level, O'*n*, of the centre of the sphere; hence, if the highest point of the vertical circle revolve to the right, as shown by the arrow, EE' will be found after revolu tion at e', at the left of the axis of revolution baE, and at a pei pendicular distance from it equal to E'n.

This done, $e'c'$ and $e'd''$ are the revolved positions of the desired tangent visual rays, and their points of tangency, c'' and d'', with the circle $d''c''b$, the revolved positions of two points of the apparent contour. By revolving the plane containing c' and d' back to ts vertical position Eab, c' and d' will revolve back about ab as an xis in arcs whose horizontal projections are $c'c$ and $d'd$, perpendicular to ab, and will give c and d as the horizontal projections of these two points of the apparent contour.

To find the vertical projection of c, for example. Consider, first, that it must be in a perpendicular to LL, through c, and that it is at a height equal to cc'' above the level O'n of the centre of the sphere. Hence on c–c' make $c'k = c'c$, and c' will be the vertical projection of the point of apparent contour whose horizontal projection is c. The vertical projection of d, not shown, in order to simplify the diagram, will be below O'n at a distance equal to $d'd$.

To find any other points of apparent contour. Intersect the sphere by any other vertical visual plane as Eq, which cuts from it the small circle whose revolved position, about pq as an axis, is $f'g'q$. In this revolution, EE' will appear at e'''; Ee''' being equal to E'n and perpendicular to Eq. The revolved visual rays $e'''f''$ and $e'''g''$ contained in this plane, give the points of contour f'' and g', whose true positions, found as before, are f and g. The vertical projection of g,g'', found also as before, is g'. Any other points of contour may be similarly found.

Finally hh', the point of contact of a *tangent* vertical visual plane, is a point of apparent contour. A similar point may be likewise found near c''. Also two tangents from E', as E'm', to the vertical projection of the sphere will be the vertical traces of visual planes perpendicular to the *vertical* plane, as Eh is to the horizontal plane. Hence their points of contact, as $m'm$, will be real points of apparen⸱ ⸱ontour on the vertical great circle through OO' and parallel to th vertical plane of projection.

[This comparatively tedious construction, which shows how greatly geometrical problems increase in complexity as we leave simple plane sided solids, shows therefore why elementary works on perspective so often confine themselves wholly to such solids, and to plane figures.]

After finding the points of apparent contour, the construction of their perspectives is the work of a moment. Thus, to find the perspective of cc'. Ec -E'c' is the visual ray from this point, and by

(58) this ray pierces the perspective plane at C, which is therefore the perspective of cc'. By finding the perspectives of the other points of apparent contour similarly, and joining them, we shall have the perspective of the sphere as seen from EE'. To remove the perspective from the projections; as before, translate the perspective plane forward to L'L', and c' an equal distance, and proceed as in (Ex. 3) to find the perspective of cc' at C' instead of at C

Remarks.—a. The method just explained is, from its nature, called the method by *secant* visual planes.

b. The student, as soon as he clearly conceives of the positions and motions explained in the preceding solution, and represented in Fig. 32, will be able to see that the vertical visual planes, as Eab, might have been revolved in two other ways. *First:* around a vertical line at E till they should be parallel to the vertical plane of projection. Then the vertical circle ab would appear vertically projected in a circle, to which tangent visual rays could be drawn from E'. *Second:* These planes might have been revolved to a similar position, each, about the vertical diameter, as at O, of the circle contained in it. In this case EE' would revolve to a new position.

c. Again: instead of *vertical* visual planes, visual planes might have been passed perpendicular to the vertical plane of projection. Any line through E' and the vertical projection of the sphere would be the vertical trace of such a plane, and it might be revolved in three ways, analogous to the three ways of revolving Eab, in order to show the circle and tangent visual rays contained in it.

The completion of the constructions thus suggested, is left as a valuable exercise for the student.

Second Method.—In this method we make use of these principles. 1°: That when a plane is tangent to the surface of a cone, it is tangent all along a straight line or *element* of that surface, from its vertex to its base. 2°: That such a plane therefore contains the vertex. 3°: That, therefore, if such a plane also contains a point in space, it will contain the straight line joining that point with the cone's vertex. 4°: That the line cut from the tangent plane by the plane of the cone's base is tangent to that base at the foot of the element of tangency (85,3°). 5°: That a cone may be circumscribed tangentially around a sphere and will then have a circle of contact with the sphere. 6°, and lastly: That the point where the *element* of tangency of a *plane and cone* intersects the *circle* of tangency of the *same cone with* a *sphere*, will be the *point of contact* of that *plane* with the *sphere*.

If now the given point in space (3°) be the point of sight, the tangent plane will also be a visual plane, and its point of contact will be a point of the apparent contour of the sphere, whose perspective will be the perspective of the sphere.

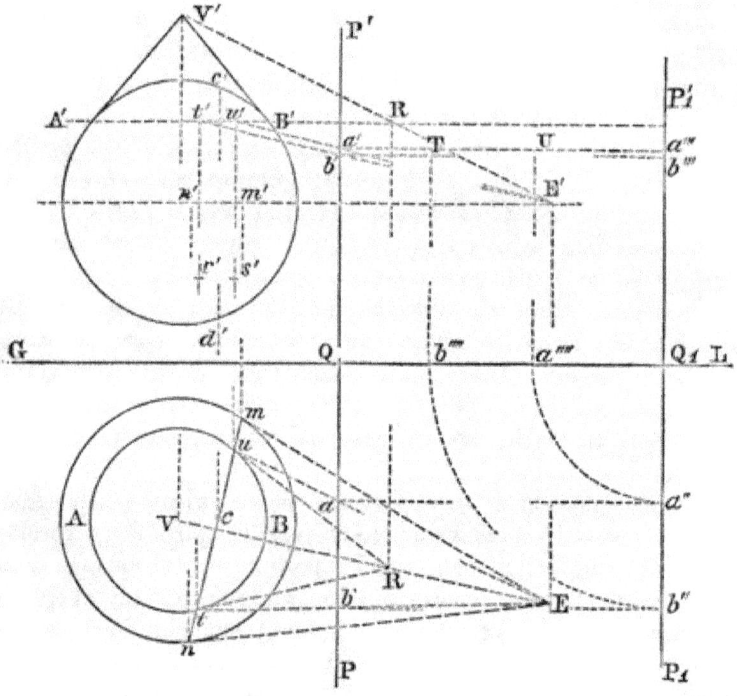

Fig. 33.

Now in Fig. 33, let Vm–A'B'd' be the given sphere, PQP' the perspective plane, and EE' the point of sight. Assume the circle A'B'–AuBt as the circle of contact of an auxiliary tangent cone (5°). The tangents V'A' and V'B' complete the vertical projection of this cone. EV–E'V', the visual ray through VV', the cone's vertex, pierces A'R', the plane of its base, at R'R–R' being found first and then projected horizontally at R (3°.) Hence by (4°) Rt and Ru are the traces of the tangent planes, to the opposite sides of the cone, upon the plane of the cone's base. Then by (4°) and (6°) tt' and uu' are points of contact of two visual planes with the sphere, and are therefore points of the apparent contour of the sphere.

This being determined, we find the perspectives of tt' and uu' as in previous cases where three planes have been used. Thus, the visual ray tE–t'E′ pierces the perspective plane at bb' ; which is translated parallel to GL, with the perspective plane, to the new position P$_1$P$_1'$, then revolved about Q$_1$P$_1'$ as an axis, into the verti cal plane at T, which is the perspective of tt'. The perspectives of other points of the apparent contour may be similarly found.

As the eye is placed, in this problem, in the horizontal plane 'E', through the centre of the sphere, the apparent contour of th sphere is evidently a vertical circle, hence nm, a straight line through t and u, and which will be perpendicular to VE, is its horizontal projection. n and m, being on the horizontal great circle of the sphere, are vertically projected at n' and m'. Two points are horizontally projected at c, at t and at u. Those at c are on the vertical great circle A′B′d', and are vertically projected at c' and d'. r' and s' are in the lines t–t' and u–u' and as far below the line $m'n'$, as t' and u' are above them.

Remarks.—a. This second method is, from its nature, called the *method of tangent visual planes.*

b. In order to familiarize the learner more effectually with this beautiful method of tangent visual planes, located by the use of auxiliary tangent cones, we will now apply it to an object of another and very different form, and with the use of three planes of projection.

Among the comparatively few large double curved surfaces occurring in the mechanic arts, whose perspectives need to be accurately constructed, are Domes, and concave Spires, &c., whose perspectives may be found as follows.

EXAMPLE 12.—**To find the Perspective of a concave Cupola-Roof.**

Let the figures with centre A and vertex A′, Fig. 34, be the projections of the cupola roof; PQP′ the original, or real position of the perspective plane, and EE′ the point of sight. The construction of A″ is, after previous similar constructions, sufficiently indicated in the figure. Then assume BtT–B′C′ as the circle of contact of an auxiliary cone, tangent to the inside of the cupola. Drawing C′v' tangent to the cupola at C′, we find v' the vertex of this cone. Then AE– v'E′, the visual ray from this vertex, pierces the plane of the cone's base at R′R (Ex. 11), hence Rt and RT are the traces, on this plane, of two planes which are tangent to this cone on elements At and AT (not drawn) and hence to the cupola at the points tt' and TT″ (Ex.11 ; 6°). The perspectives of these points are t'' and T″, found by making c''T″ $=$Qc, &c. (Ex. 6, Rem. *b.*)

At the base of the cupola is a round edged band, three points of which, mm'; nn' and r' it is sufficient to find in perspective, as at

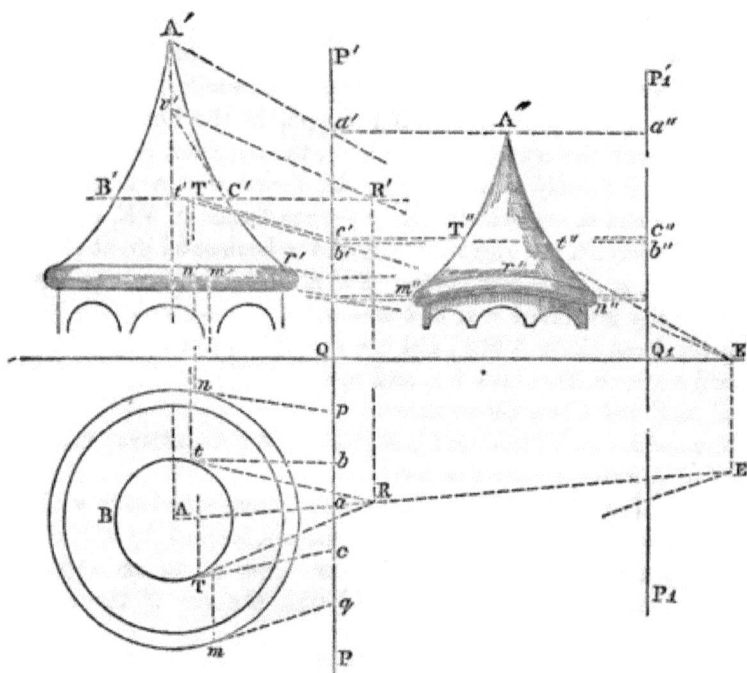

FIG. 34.

m'', n'', and r''. Through these points the perspective of the cupola can be sketched.

CHAPTER VII.

PERSPECTIVES OF SHADOWS.

General Principles and Illustrations.

89. Perspectives of shadows, like those of objects, are readily found from their projections, by the method of visual rays already explained.

But shadows, being obviously not independent of the bodies casting them, require a little separate preliminary study, to show how they are found when those bodies are given.

90. The shadow of a body on any surface, is that portion of that surface from which light is excluded by the body.

A shadow is known when its bounding edge, called *the line of shadow*, is known.

91. Rays of light from a very distant source, as the sun, fall upon any terrestrial object in *parallel straight lines*.

92. Any ray which is intercepted by the given body will, evidently, if produced through the body, pierce the shadow within its boundary. Any ray, not intercepted by the body, will evidently pierce the supposed surface containing the shadow, beyond the edge of the shadow. Hence *the line of shadow is the shadow of that line on the given body, at all points of which the rays are tangent to the body.*

This line of contact of rays, separates the illuminated from the unilluminated portion of the given body, and is called the *line of shade*.

93. Since the line of shadow is thus the shadow of the line of shade, the latter must always be found first.

The line of shade, from which shadows are determined, is found in the same general manner as the line of apparent contour, from which perspectives are determined; viz. by *inspection* on most plane sided bodies, and by the aid of tangent *rays of light*, or tangent *planes of rays of light*, on curved surfaces.

5

94. Practically, shadows are found, a point at a time, and any one point in a line of shadow is where a ray of light, from some point in the line of shade of a given body, pierces the surface receiving the shadow.

Hence it is obvious that the *form* of a shadow will depend both on the form of the body casting it and that of the surface receiving it, and also on the direction of the light; while *the method of find ing it* will depend only on the form of the surface receiving it.

95. Finally : *To find a shadow*, we must have given, by their projections, 1*st*. The body casting it; 2*nd*. The surface receiving it; 3*rd*. The direction of the light. These given, we may then construct, 1*st*. The line of shade on the given body; 2*nd*. The shadow determined by that line of shade. This done, we can at last construct the perspective of the shadow.

Problems of perspectives of shadows being thus obviously somewhat tedious and complex, only a few simple and generally useful ones are here inserted, as an introduction to the subject.

The shadows which most frequently occur in perspective drawings such as are made largely for pictorial effect, are the shadows cast by lines in various positions, on the ground, and on the walls and roofs of buildings. The following principles and examples, therefore, give elementary illustrations of the operations necessary in finding such shadows.

96. Let AB, Fig. 35, be a slender vertical rod or wire, and let LR represent a ray of light drawn through its upper extremity, B, and piercing the horizontal plane GH at R. Then R will be the shadow of the point B. But the point, as A, in which a line meets a surface, is a point of the shadow of that line on that surface. Hence AR is the shadow of AB on the horizontal plane GH. But BA being vertical, AR is also the horizontal projection of the ray BR. Hence, *the shadow of a vertical line on the horizontal plane is in the direction of the horizontal projection of the light.*

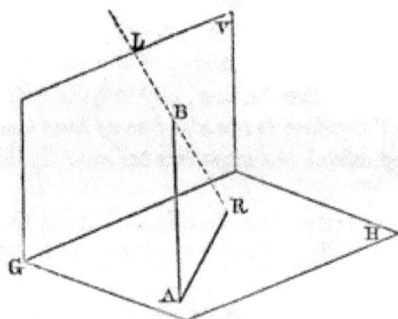

FIG. 35.

97. By operating in a precisely similar manner upon a line perpendicular to the vertical plane GV, it will be found that the sha-

dow of such a line upon the vertical plane, will be in the direction of the vertical projection of the rays of light.

98. Since the rays of light are parallel, it is clear that *the shadow of a vertical line on the vertical plane, will, itself, be a vertical line ;* likewise, the shadow of a horizontal line on a horizontal plane, will be parallel to the line, and, generally, for the same reason, if a line be parallel to any plane, its shadow on that plane will be parallel to the line itself. Hence, also, *the shadows of parallel lines on the same plane, will be parallel to each other.*

99. If the same line casts a shadow on both planes of projection, the shadows on the two planes must meet the ground line at the same point. Thus in Fig. 36, let AC be a vertical line, long enough to cast its shadow partly on each plane of projection. Then R, where the shadow AR leaves the horizontal plane GH, must be the beginning of the shadow RT on the vertical plane. For all the rays CT, BR, &c., from points on AC, being parallel, form a plane *called a plane of rays*, of which AR and RT are the traces, and it has already been shown (78), that the two traces of the same plane must meet the ground line at the same point.

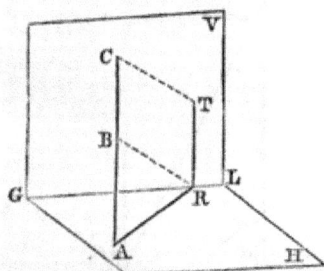

FIG. 36.

Finally, in general, if the shadow of any line, as the top edge of a roof, falls on both of any two intersecting surfaces, as the front and side of another building, these two shadows will meet at a common point on the edge dividing those surfaces. Hence, *when we have the complete shadow on one such surface, this common point gives us one point of the shadow on the other surface.*

EXAMPLE 13.—To find the **Perspective of the Shadow of a Square Abacus upon a Square Pillar.**

The method of two planes is here employed, GL, Fig. 37, being the first, and G'L' the second position of the ground line. The construction of the perspective of the pillar and its cap (abacus) is not shown, it being exactly like many previous constructions. Also, no more of the vertical projection of the object is made than is necessary in finding its perspective, and shadows.

Rays of light, like other lines, being indicated, in position, by their projections, let A*l* and A'L' be the projections of the ray through the front right hand upper corner, AA', of the abacus

This ray pierces the horizontal plane at l, whose vertical projection, which must be in the ground line (45), is L'. Therefore the point

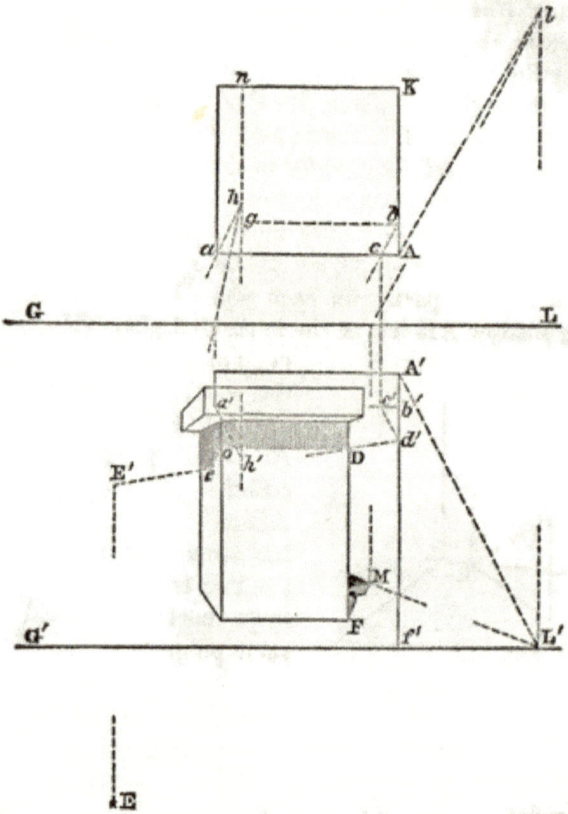

FIG. 37.

itself is at l, which is therefore the shadow of AA' on the horizontal lane.

The shadow of the lower front edge, aA–$a'b'$, of the abacus, upon the front of the pillar, will be parallel to itself (98). When the direction of a line is known, one point in it is sufficient to determine it; hence, to find this shadow, it is only necessary to pass a ray, as cb–$c'd'$, through any point, as cc', of the lower front edge of the abacus, and to find where this ray pierces the front face of the pillar, as at b,d'. In this case, by drawing the ray through b, in plan, the point of shadow, b,d', is made to fall on the right hand vertical edge, b–$b'f'$, of the pillar. A line through d', and parallel to $a'b'$, will be the vertical projection of the shadow of aA-$a'b'$. Drawing the visual ray $d'E'$, its intersection, D, with DF, the perspective of $b'f'$, will be the perspective of d'; and as the shadow is parallel to the perspective plane, its perspective will be parallel to itself (69, a), that is a horizontal line through D.

Next, drawing the ray ah-$a'h'$, we find hh', the shadow of aa' the lower, front, left hand corner of the abacus, on the side surface, gn, of the pillar, whose vertical projection is a line through h' equal and parallel to $b'f'$. The visual ray, hE-$h'E'$, from hh' gives its perspective, e. Then eo is the shadow of a small portion of aA-$a'b'$ upon the left side of the pillar.

Now for the shadow on the horizontal plane. The shadow of the point AA' is l, where the ray Al-$A'L'$ pierces that plane. The vertical projection of l is L' (45), and the visual ray, lE-$L'E'$, therefore gives M as the perspective of the point lL'. In the same way, find the shadows of the points A, b' and bb', and join the latter shadow with F. The shadow of A'-AK will be parallel to that line, and will begin at l. Hence, as will fully appear on making the construction, $L'E'$ will also be the vertical projection of the visual ray from the shadow of K. Hence ME', up to DF, is the visible portion of the perspective of the shadow of A'-AK.

EXAMPLE 14.—To find the Perspective of the Shadow of any triangular Pyramid upon the Horizontal Plane.

In this problem we shall employ the simple principles, that the shadow of the point where any number of lines meet is the point where the shadows of those lines meet; and that the point in which a line pierces the horizontal plane is a point of its shadow on that plane.

The method by two planes is employed, and the construction of the perspective of the pyramid, being the same as in many previous problems, is briefly indicated in the diagram, only, Fig. 38.

Let ABC be the plan of the base of the pyramid, and V, that of its vertex. V'-$A'B'C'$ is the vertical projection of the pyramid This vertical projection, being shown in full on the original position of the vertical, or perspective plane, only its points, $A''B''C''$ and V'', are shown, in the same relative position, on the translated position of the same plane, whose ground line is $G'L'$. In fact, after becoming quite at home in the subject of perspective, the student will see that $A'B'C'$-V' might have been omitted altogether; and, in general, that often only points, and not lines, of the projections of objects need be shown, in order to find their perspectives.

Having, as in previous problems, found v-abc, the perspective of the pyramid, draw the *ray of light* VR–V'R' which pierces the horizontal plane at R, projected back from R' in the ground line.

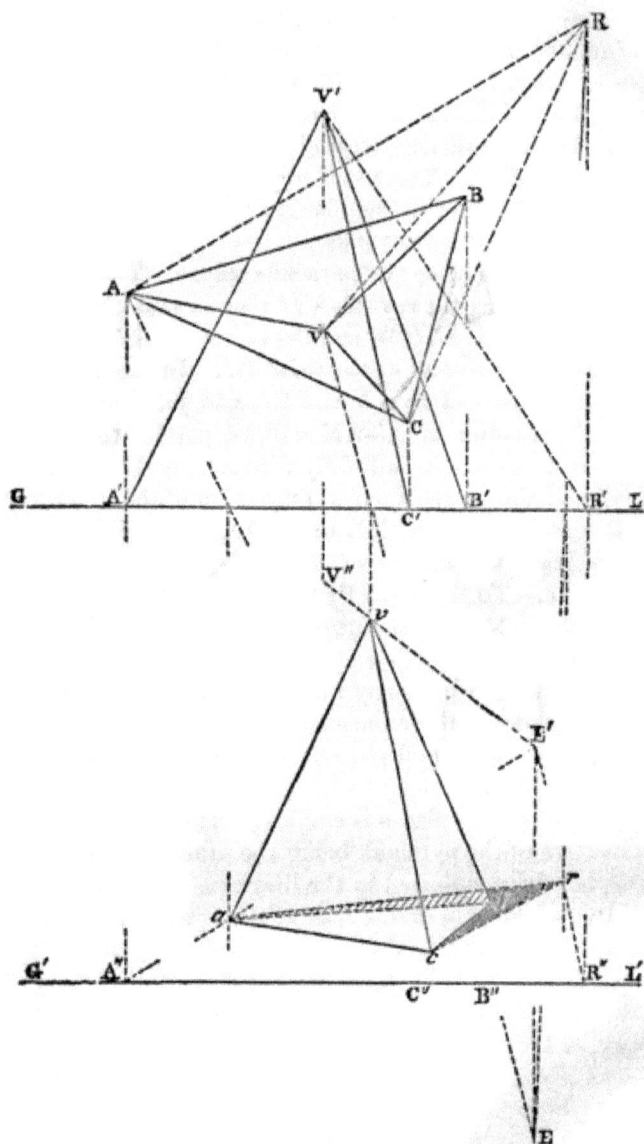

FIG. 38.

Then R is the shadow of VV' on the horizontal plane, and A and

C being their own shadows—(96—and the second principle above stated—)RA and RC are the shadows of VA and VC. Then, drawing the *visual ray* RE–R″E′, we find r for the perspective of RR″; R″ being the vertical projection, R′, in its second position. Hence ra and rc are the perspectives of the shadows RA and RC, which limit the shadow whose perspective was required.

. EXAMPLE 15.—**To find the Perspective of the Shadow of Dormer Window upon a Roof.**

In this concluding example of shadows, found by primitive methods, we will, for further variety, employ the method by three planes. Again, this example involves the shadows of lines in three different positions, upon a slanting surface, and affords the most instructive variety with the fewest lines. Moreover, as the shadows of lines are determined by the shadows of points in them, and as the shadow of a point is the same—and similarly found—whether the point be on a straight line or curve, a careful study of this and the two preceding examples should enable the student to find the projections and perspective of any ordinary shadow.

First, now, in Fig. 39, to find the *projections* of the windows and roof. To avoid unnecessary lines, only a small portion of one slope of a roof is shown, of which ABCD is the plan, CDC‴″D‴ is the auxiliary elevation, showing the true size of the front of the dormer, and A′B′C′D′–C′D″, found as in Ex. 10, is the principal elevation. G and F are the plans of the vertical edges of the dormer, whose true heights I″G″ and J″F″ appear in vertical projection at I′G′ and J′F′. The vertical projection, E′, of the peak of the gable, FEG, is found on the projecting line ENE′, by laying off NE′ equal to its height, N″E″, above the horizontal plane. Then draw E′G′ and E′F′. NK′ parallel to B′C″, is evidently the trace on the roof, of a vertical plane through the ridge EK–E′K′, which therefore meets the roof in this trace at K′, whose horizontal projection is K. The points HH′ and LL′ are similarly found, and then joined with KK′.

Next, to find the *projections* of the shadows on the roof. Le FP and F′P′ be the projections of a ray of light to which all the other rays are parallel. The shadow of the vertical edge, F–F′J′, will fall in FS–J′S′, the trace on the roof of a vertical plane of rays (99) through that edge.

The ray FP–F′P′ meets this trace at P′, which is then horizontally projected at P, and FP–J′ P′ is the shadow of F–J′F′. Then PP′ being the shadow of FF′ (94), and LL′ being its own shadow (96), LP–L′P′ is (geometrically, for this shadow is unreal), the shadow of FL–F'L'. The shadows of parallel lines, on the same plane,

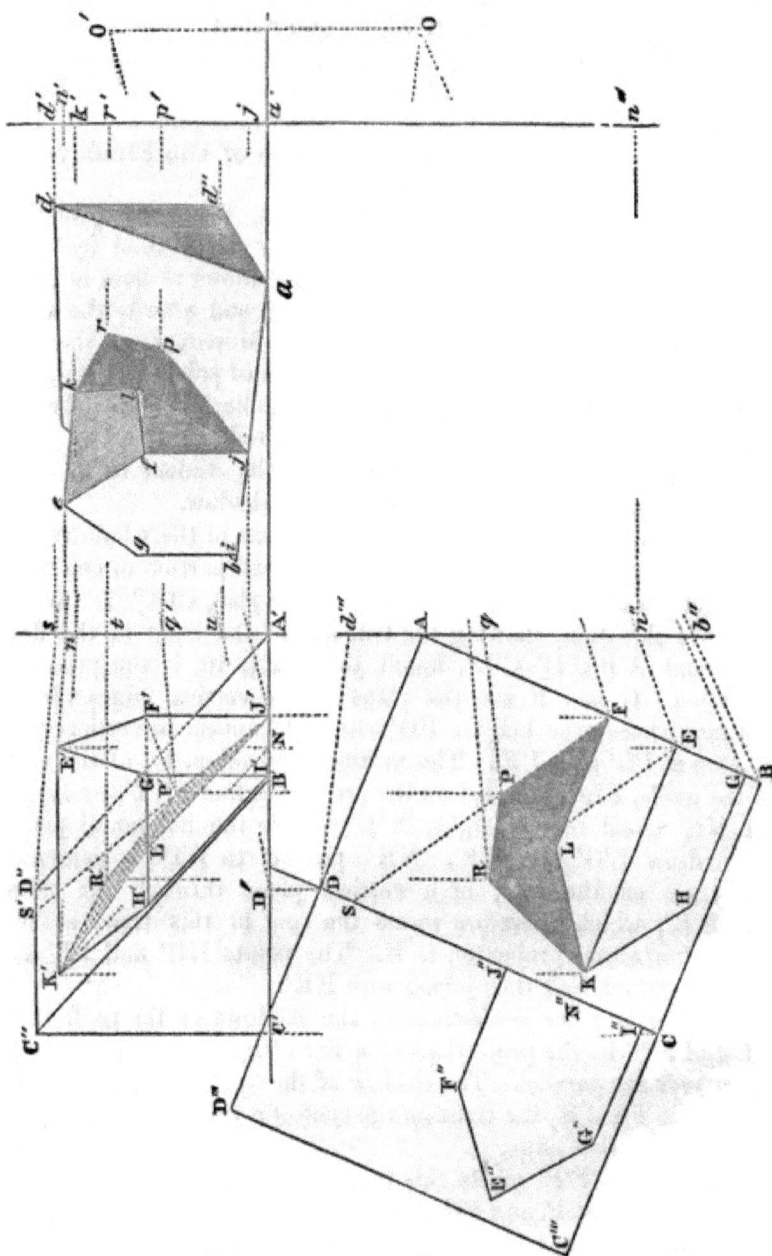

FIG. 39.

being parallel (98), KR-K'R' the shadow of EK-E'K', is parallel to LP-L'P' and is limited at R by the ray ER. R' is then projected from R. Finally, by drawing RP-R'P', we have the shadow of EF-E'F'.

Lastly, to find the *perspective* of the roof and shadows, whose projections have just been completed. Let $b^x A's$ be the original, and $a'd'$ the translated position of the perspective plane; and let OO' be the point of sight. This construction scarcely needs any explanation, exactly similar ones having been often fully explained already. One or two points only are mentioned, to acquaint the learner with the abbreviations which are made in the construction of the figure. To find e, for example. Draw the ray EO-E'O' and from its intersection, n, with the perspective plane, draw nn', parallel to the ground line; then make $n'e = n''A'$, and e will be the perspective of EE', since this is obviously equivalent to translating n'' to n''', and revolving it, as in the previous unabridged constructions.

Having found d, the perspective of DD', in the same way, also f, and g, the lines dd', fj and gi can immediately be drawn perpendicular to the ground line, since they are the perspectives of vertical lines. dd'' is limited at d'', simply by drawing D'O' to u, and ud'', parallel to the ground line. fj and gi are limited by their intersection with ab. a is the perspective of the point AA', which is its own perspective, it being in the perspective plane, and $a'a = A'A$.

The perspectives of the points of shadow are found in the same manner. Thus, to find p, draw the ray PO-P'O' to qq', and the line of translation $q'p'$, and make $p'p = A'q$, which will give p, the perspective of PP'. Drawing jp, finding r, the perspective of RR', as p was just found, then drawing pr, and rk, we shall have the complete perspective of the shadow on the roof.

PART II.

DERIVATIVE METHODS.

CHAPTER I.

GENERAL PRINCIPLES AND ILLUSTRATIONS.

100. In all the problems of PART I., we have found the perspective of every point by one and the same *primitive and natural method*, which consists in finding where a visual ray (actually represented) through any given point, pierces the perspective plane.

This method is primitive, and peculiarly the natural one, because it manifestly embodies the simplest geometrical definition of the perspective of a given point, viz. that it is where a visual ray from that point pierces the perspective plane (35).

It is true, that in the practical application of this method, having revolved the perspective plane directly back into the horizontal plane, a difficulty arose, as in Figs. 16 and 17, from the confounding together of the projections and the perspective in one place on the paper. This difficulty led, *first:* to the translation forward of the perspective plane, till it could be revolved back into the horizontal plane so as to bring the perspective below the projections, as in Fig. 19; *second:* to the use of three distinct planes, as in Figs. 22, etc., where the difficulty of confusion of figures was obviated most completely. But these merely particular *graphical methods* f applying the method of visual rays, evidently do not alter the method itself, and we repeat, that all the problems of PART I. were solved by the primitive method of finding where visual rays, actually represented, through given points, pierced the perspective plane.

101. All problems whatever, in perspective, might be readily solved in this simple and beautiful manner; but by inspection of the perspectives thus found, certain peculiarities may be discovered, which, on examination, lead to other methods, hence called deriva-

tive ; or, because the visual rays are no longer represented, com
paratively, artificial methods.

The advantages of knowing several methods, which will soon
appear, are chiefly two : 1° Abbreviation of the operations of construction.   2° Provision of checks upon inaccuracy.

It has already been shown by experimental proof, in previous
constructions, that any lines, whether vertical or horizontal, which
are parallel to the perspective plane, have their perspectives parallel
to each other, and to the lines themselves.   Also that the perspectives of all lines which are perpendicular to the perspective plane,
meet at the vertical projection of the eye. (Fig. 16.)   These two
results have also already been separately proved to be true, (Ex.
1. *Rems. a,b.*) but by now considering them in connexion with a few
others, we shall arrive at a body of principles by which perspectives of objects can be found by the derivative methods, which it
is the object of this second " PART " to explain.

102. In standing on a vast plane, such as a natural plain, its
remotest visible limit appears as a horizontal line on a level with
the eye.   The reason of this is evident from Fig. 40.   Let E be the

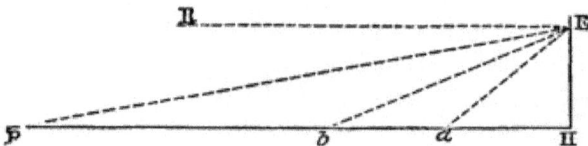

FIG. 40.

place of the observer's eye, looking forward in the direction ER,
parallel to the ground HP.   In taking successive points on the
ground, as *a, b,* and P, at greater and greater distances from the observer, standing at H, the visual rays *a*E . . . . PE, &c., become more
and more nearly horizontal, and finally, when a ray comes from an
indefinitely remote point on the ground, its direction cannot be distinguished from that of the horizontal visual ray ER.   Hence, as the
apparent position of objects depends on the direction of the visual
rays entering the eye from them, *the very remote limit of any level
plane appears as a horizontal line, on a level with the eye.*

103. The indefinitely remote limit of a natural plain, or horizontal geometrical plane, is called the *horizon ;* hence a line parallel
to the ground line, and through the vertical projection of the point
of sight, is the *perspective of the horizon.*

Such a line is called *the horizontal line*, or the horizon of the picture.

104. It follows from this, that the remotest visible limit of *all lines in such a plane*, that is of *all horizontal lines*, will appear to be in *the* " horizontal " line, which represents the remotest limit of this plane.

105. Now the remotest visible limit of the plane supposed, is literally its *vanishing line*, and, likewise, the remotest visible point of any line in that plane, is its *vanishing point*. The representation of this line, or point, on the perspective plane, is the perspective of such line or point, and is, according to the last two articles, a line or point on the perspective plane, and at the height of the eye.

106. The *perspective* of a vanishing line or point being of constant use in the construction of perspectives, while the original indefinitely distant *real* vanishing line, or point, is not, the former is, for brevity, itself termed the vanishing line, or point.

Hence we have these principles: 1°. *The vanishing line of any horizontal plane, is a horizontal line, drawn on the perspective plane and at the height of the eye.* 2°. *Any horizontal line has its vanishing point in the* " *horizontal* " *line.*

107. Similar reasoning might be applied, and with corresponding conclusions, to vertical, or oblique planes, but as we do not find in Nature real planes of indefinite extent, everyway, in these positions, it will be sufficient to consider the vanishing points of *lines*, only, in any direction.

108. The visual ray from the indefinitely distant, or remotest visible limit of an unlimited line, will evidently appear to be parallel to that line, and the intersection of this ray with the perspective plane, is the perspective of that remote or *real* vanishing point. *This intersection itself* (106) *is practically called the vanishing point*, in making perspective drawings; and will be so called in the following pages. Also, a visual ray which is parallel to one line, is arallel to all others, which are parallel to that one. Hence *to find the vanishing point* of any line or *group of parallel lines*, we have the following rule. *Find where a visual ray, parallel to the given lines, pierces the perspective plane ; the point thus found will be the required vanishing point.*

109. *Illustration.* Let PP, Fig. 41, represent the perspective plane, and L,L,L, three parallel lines in any direction. These lines will appa- rently meet, and so may be considered as meeting, at an indefinitely great distance, and the visual ray VE from their distant apparent intersection, will, for any short distance, as EV, be sensibly parallel

to them. But V, the intersection of this ray with the perspective plane, is the perspective of that intersection. That is, V is the vanishing point of L,L,L.

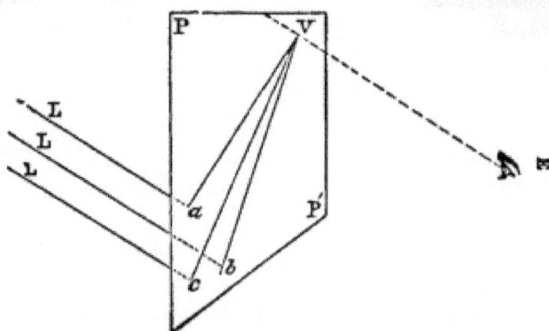

FIG. 41.

Observe finally, that as *parallel lines themselves* appear to meet at their indefinitely remote point, so their *perspectives* will meet at their vanishing point on the perspective plane, which is the perspective of their *real* vanishing point in space. Thus, if aV, bV, and cV are the perspectives of L,L,L, they will meet at V.

110. In general, if any number of lines meet at any point, their *perspectives* will evidently meet at the *perspective of that point*.

EXAMPLE 1.—Let it be required to find the vanishing point of several Telegraph Wires which go over a hill.

In Fig. 42 let AA′ and BB′ be two successive poles, carrying two wires. AB is the plan of both of these wires. Let CC′ and DD′ be another pair of poles, of a line of single wire, and let EE′ be the position of the eye. Then EV, parallel to AB or CD, and E′V′, parallel to A′B′ or C′D′, are the projections of the visual ray, parallel to these wires, and therefore giving the perspective of an indefinitely remote point upon them. This ray meets the perspective plane at V′ (58), which is therefore the vanishing point at which the perspectives of the wires will meet.

111. From the general case just considered, in illustration of the general principle of (108) let us proceed to find the location of the vanishing points of groups of parallels, having particular positions with respect to the perspective plane.

First. It follows directly from the rule (108), that *all lines which are parallel to the perspective plane have no vanishing point.* Hence their perspectives will be parallel to themselves. That is, the perspectives of vertical lines, for example, will be vertical, as

seen in (Fig. 16, etc., PART I.)   Also, if lines are parallel to the
ground line, their perspectives will be parallel to the ground line,
as also seen in Fig. 16.

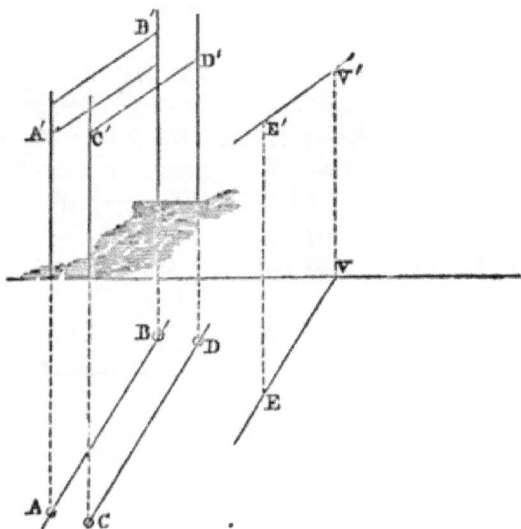

FIG. 42.

Second. It also follows from (108), that all horizontal lines nave
their vanishing points in *the* horizontal line, or horizon (103).

112. In particular, among *horizontal* lines, we notice those which
are also perpendicular to the perspective plane; and those which
make an angle of 45° with the perspective plane. The former are
called *perpendiculars*, and the latter, *diagonals*.

EXAMPLE 2.—To find the vanishing point of a Perpendicular, and of a Diagonal.

See Fig. 43, where Dc is the ground line, EE' the point of sight,
and D'A the horizontal line.

By (48), when a line is perpendicular to the vertical plane, its
vertical projection is a point, and its horizontal projection, a line,
perpendicular to the ground line. Therefore *ab* is the horizontal,
and *a'* the vertical projection of a perpendicular, at the height *aa'*
above the horizontal plane. Likewise E*e* is the horizontal, and E'
the vertical projection of a visual ray, parallel to *ab-a'*. This
visual ray pierces the perspective, or vertical plane at E', which
is therefore the vanishing point of *ab-a'* and of all perpendiculars
(108) while EE' remains as the place of the eye.

113. The point E′, the vertical projection of the point of sight, is usually known among artists as the *centre of the picture ;* since in a picture of equal interest throughout, it should be in the centre, of the horizontal width, at least, of the canvas. Therefore we say that *the vanishing point of perpendiculars is at the centre of the picture.* E is often called the station point.

114. To return now to the diagonal. By (51), when a line is parallel to the horizontal plane only, its vertical projection is parallel to the ground line, hence (112), making $ac = ab$, $abc = acb =$ 45°, and bc will be the horizontal projection of a diagonal through the point b, $a′$ and $a′c′$ will be its vertical projection. Then ED–E′D′ is the parallel visual ray which pierces the perspective plane (58), at D′. Hence D′ is the vanishing point of bc–$a′c′$ and of all other diagonals (108).

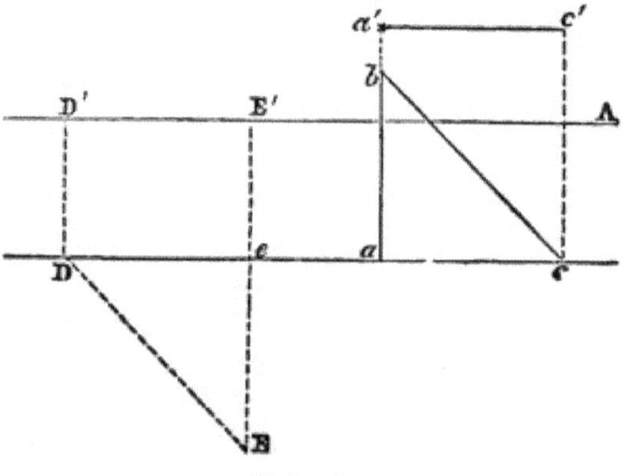

FIG. 43.

115. Observe in Fig. 43, that $Ee = eD = E′D′$, that is, *the distance from the centre of the picture to the vanishing point of diagonals is equal to the distance of the eye from the perspective plane.* Hence, having either **E** *or* D′ given, with E′, we can find the other of these points. Thus, having E′ and D,′ make $eE = E′D′$ which gives E; and having E and E′ given, make $E′D′ = Ee$, which gives D′.

116. *The point in which a line pierces the perspective plane, is a point of its perspective ;* for the visual ray from that point pierces the perspective plane at its outset. Also, as follows from (109), the vanishing point of a line is a point of its perspective. Moreover, two points determine a straight line, hence *the perspective of a straight line is a line joining its vanishing point with the point where it pierces the perspective plane.*

Thus, in Fig. 44, the perpendicular ab–a' pierces the perspective plane at a'; and the diagonal, at c'; hence, if we draw $a'E'$, it will be the perspective of this perpendicular, and if we draw $c'D'$, it will be the perspective of the diagonal, bc–$a'c'$.

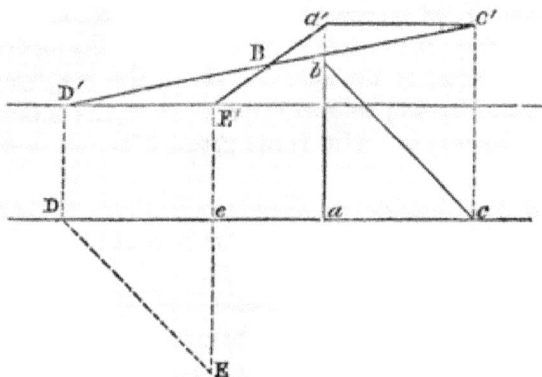

FIG. 44.

See also a pictorial illustration in Fig. 41, for lines in any direction. There the three parallels meet the perspective plane at a, b, and c, and V being their vanishing point (109) aV, bV, and cV are their perspectives.

117. It follows from (110) that if two lines intersect at a point, their perspectives will intersect at the perspective of that point, that is, *the intersection of the perspectives of two lines, is the perspective of the intersection of the lines themselves.* Hence in Fig. 44, B, the intersection of the perspectives of the perpendicular ab–a' and diagonal bc–$a'c'$, is the perspective of the point b, a' from which both of these lines originated.

Particular Derivative Methods.

118. It is now apparent that, by the principles of (116) and (117) the perspective of any point, and hence of any object, can be found without the use of any visual rays.

Derivative methods, then, consist in substituting for the visual ray from any given point, *any two* lines containing that point; and in finding their perspectives, by joining their intersections with the perspective plane, with their vanishing points (116). The intersection of the perspectives of these lines will then be the perspective of the given point (117).

119. Since all parallel lines have the same vanishing point (108)

it will obviously abridge the constructions to use auxiliary lines in parallel sets. This being clear, it further appears, that no auxiliary lines are so universally simple and convenient as *diagonals* and *perpendiculars ;* first: because the centre of the picture, which is always given, being the vanishing point of perpendiculars, no vanishing point need be *constructed* for them ; second, because the distance D'E' from the centre of the picture to the vanishing point of diagonals is equal to the distance, *e*E, of the eye from the perspective plane, Fig. 43 ; so that if the latter is given, the former is immediately known, and if it is not given, E'D' *can be assumed at pleasure.*

Foremost therefore among derivative methods, is the method of diagonals and perpendiculars, as explained and illustrated in (112 to 117) all of which is based on (110).

120. The only other derivative method, which need be mentioned, is one which is applicable to bodies bounded by straight lines, which are arranged in parallel groups, as in a square prism. In this case, the lines of the object itself may be put in perspective by (116). The intersections of their perspectives will then be the perspectives of the corners of the object.

Derivative methods, exclusively, are generally used in connection with two planes, only, of projection.

121. We will now close this chapter with three fundamental illustrative examples, showing, *first,* how to find the perspective of any line whatever by its vanishing point and point of intersection with the perspective plane ; *second,* how to find the perspective of any object by the method of diagonals and perpendiculars ; and, *third,* how to find the perspective of a plane sided object by finding the vanishing and intersection points of its own edges.

EXAMPLE 3.—To find the Perspective of a Straight Line in any position, oblique to both planes of projection, by its vanishing point and intersection with the perspective lane.

Figs. 45 and 46. To familiarize the student more fully with this problem, and so to render the conception of positions in space, corresponding to given projections, more easy, two different lines have been taken in the above figures, while for more ready comparison, like points are lettered with the same letters in both figures. Accordingly, *ab–a'b'*, in both cases, is a line behind the perspective plane, as usual. Its extremity *aa'* is at the distance *ac behind the perspective plane*, and height, *a'c above the horizontal plane.* *b,* being in the ground line, is the horizontal projection of that point of the given line, which is in the vertical plane, that is, the point b'. That is $ab–a'b'$ pierces the vertical, or perspective plane at b' which is therefore one point of the perspective of this line (116).

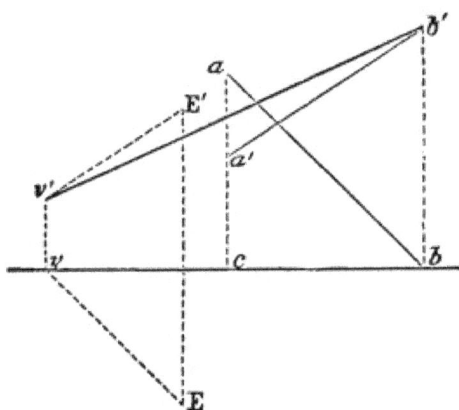

FIG. 45.

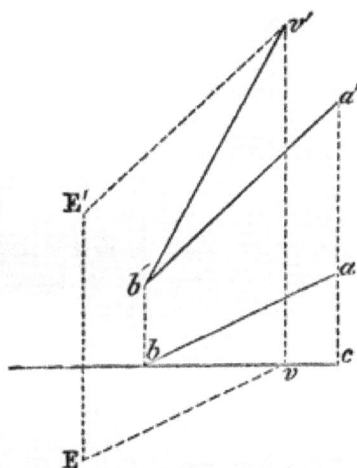

FIG. 46.

Again: $Ev–E'v'$, parallel to $ab–a'b'$, is the parallel visual ray from the infinitely distant point of $ab–a'b'$ (108). Hence v', where this ray pierces the perspective plane, is the perspective of that infinitely remote point. That is, v' is the vanishing point (106) of $ab–a'b'$. Hence by (116) $v'b'$ is the perspective of $ab–a'b'$.

Remarks. a.—As v' is the perspective of an infinitely distant point on $ab-a'b'$, $v'b'$ is the perspective of $ab-a'b'$ produced to an infinite length, from bb', back from the perspective plane.

b. As a further exercise, let the student take lines in other positions. Thus in Fig. 45 let the given line have such a position that $a'b'$ shall be its horizontal, and ab its vertical projection, and then find its perspective, as before.

EXAMPLE 4.—**To construct the Perspective of a Tower and Spire, by diagonals and perpendiculars.**

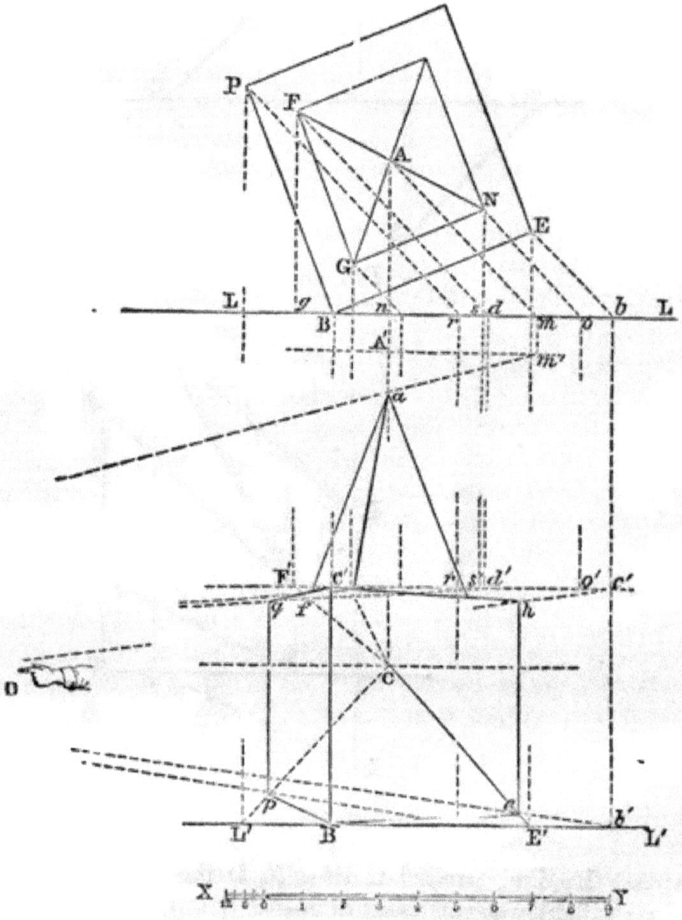

FIG. 47.

Fig. 47, let PBE be the plan of the tower, and FGN of the spire whose vertex is A. Let LL be the ground line, taken through the corner B, which indicates the real position of the perspective plane, L'L' indicates the position of the perspective plane after translation forward. CD is the horizon, and C the centre of the picture. The vanishing point of diagonals is assumed on CD, at the left of C, and, in this case, beyond the limits of the picture.

[This preliminary explanation is substantially common to most of the following problems, and is therefore to be understood though not repeated.]

Since the vertical edge at B is in the perspective plane, it is its own perspective, hence its vertical projection, B'C', which shows the true height of the tower, is also its perspective. To find the perspective of either of the other visible vertical edges, as the one at E, draw the diagonal Eb from the corner, E, of the base of the tower. E'b' is the vertical projection of this diagonal, since it is in the horizontal plane; it pierces the perspective plane at b', and b'D (D meaning the vanishing point of diagonals, not shown) is its perspective. Em, the perpendicular from the same point E, pierces the perspective plane at E', and E'C is its perspective. Hence e, the intersection of b'D and E'C, is the perspective of E, considered as in the lower base of the tower. p is found from P in a precisely similar manner. Then draw pB' and B'e.

To find any point, as h, of the top of the tower. Eb, considered as the diagonal from the point E in the top of the tower, pierces the perspective plane at the true height of the tower, that is at c', in the horizontal line through C', since diagonals are always horizontal lines (112). Then c'D is the perspective of this diagonal. The perspective of the perpendicular from the upper point, E, is not needed, since the perspective of the vertical edge at E is known to be a vertical line through e. Hence h, the intersection of eh, drawn perpendicular to the ground line, with c'D, is the perspective of the top corner of the tower at E. q is found in the same manner. Then draw qC' and C'h.

To find any point, as f, in the perspective of the base of the spire r' is the perspective of F, and the plane of the base of the spire is the same as that of the top of the tower; hence the diagonal, Fd, and the perpendicular, Fg, pierce the perspective plane in the horizontal line through C', at d' and F', respectively. Then d'D is the perspective of Fd, and F'C, that of Fg ; and f, the intersection of these perspectives, is the perspective of F. The top of the tower being above CD, the level of the eye, the base of the spire is invisible. The perspectives of G and N are found in the manner just described.

Finally, the height of A'm' above the ground line, represents the height of the top of the spire. Then the diagonal, Am, and perpendicular, An, pierce the perspective plane at m' and A'. m'D is the perspective of Am, and A'C, that of An. Hence a is the perspective of A. Now join a with f, and the other points of the base of the spire, limiting the lines thus drawn by qC' and C'h, and the required perspective will be complete.

122. Various miscellaneous points, which naturally arise in the mind of a beginner, are most conveniently disposed of here, after the progress thus far made with primitive and derivative methods. They are therefore discussed in the following—

Remarks.—a. The statements in (101) can now be made more intelligible. *First. Derivative methods abridge the labor of construction:* first :—through the *partial omission of the projections*, as seen in the above example, where the vertical projection was not required, because the *auxiliary lines*, being *horizontal*, will always pierce the perspective plane at the height of the points from which they are drawn, and these heights can always be indicated by setting them off, as $b'c'$ was, equal to B'C', the real known height of the top of. the tower ; second :— by the *provision of common vanishing points* for all parallel lines, so that, 1°,—only one other point in each indefinite line, need be found ; and 2°,—so that any particular point, as h, on such a line, can be found by a single auxiliary, as c'D.

Second. Derivative methods also conduce to accuracy ; first :— by *providing against errors arising from very acute intersections* in the lines of construction. See PART I., Fig. 19, where, though the intersection at A is well defined, that at F, and especially at the perspectives of c'' and d'' (not shown) are not. Whenever, therefore, another method fails to give well-defined intersections, that of diagonals and perpendiculars will be generally found available. Second: by the *provision against distortion of apparent proportions*, which is afforded by vanishing points. It is a matter of familiar experience, that all receding parallels in the same group appear to vanish at the same point, and in a drawing, where vanishing points are employed, their perspectives will likewise vanish. But if no vanishing points are used, so that the perspective of each line of a parallel set is found *independently of the others*, by finding two points in it, it may happen that these perspectives, if produced, will not meet at one point. Errors in the true *relative direction* of perspectives are far more offensive to the eye than the less obvious errors in the absolute place of single points.

b. The disuse of vertical projections which the method of diagonals and perpendiculars allows, is another advantage of that method over those in which the auxiliary lines might not be horizontal.

c. The question naturally occurs to a practical inquirer, "how shall I represent an object of *given dimensions,* viewed from a *given distance,* and in a *given direction."* See Fig. 47. If in practice the distances from P and E to the observer be measured, the exact *relative position* of the tower and the observer will be known, and so can be laid down on paper. This done, we can, from a given position, look straight forward towards the centre of an object, as shown by the line CA in the figure, or we can turn and look towards the right or left of the centre so as to see the object partially by a sidewise glance of the eye.

The *clearest view* is obtained in the former case, but in any case the perspective plane is supposed to be perpendicular to the direction of vision. Thus, if the spectator at E, Fig. 48, observe O,

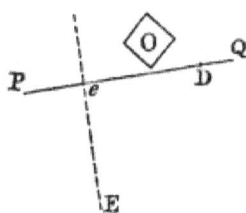

among other things, while looking in the direction E*e*, the perspective plane PQ should be perpendicular to E*e ;* simply because this is its simplest and most natural position.

This being understood, make *e*D = *e*E, to find the vanishing point of diagonals

FIG. 48.

(115) or, in Fig. 47, lay off from *n*, on A*n*C produced, a distance equal to CD, to find the position of the observer, or horizontal projection of the point of sight, often called *the station point*(113).

d. But, further, in representing large objects truly, all these *dimensions* and *distances,* just spoken of, must be reduced uniformly, so as to be shown at all, and in true proportion, on paper. In other words they must be drawn to a scale.

For example, let it be supposed that in Fig. 47, all given parts are to be shown on a uniform scale of five feet to an inch, *i.e. five feet* on the real object, to *one inch* on the drawing. On any straight line as XY, lay off two or more inches, and divide each inch, as shown, into five equal parts. Each of these parts will therefore *represent* one foot, and hence, in connexion with the drawing, *may be called* one foot. Let the left hand one of these feet be subdivided into twelfths (fourths only are shown) which will be inches. Any other scale is made in a similar manner. Having such a scale, its zero point is at the right hand end of the divided foot. If then, the tower is 5 ft. 9 ins. square, as at BP and

BE, extend the dividers from the point marked five to the 3 inch point between 6 and 12, which will be five feet nine inches, on a scale of five feet to one inch. So, if the object be 11 ft. 6 ins. high, make the line $A'm'$ at this perpendicular distance from the ground line $L'L'$.

It thus appears that in using any scale, thus constructed and numbered, no calculations need be made, since we take up in th dividers the same number of *scale* feet and inches, that there are of *real* feet and inches in any given line to be represented. The question of *Rem. c* is thus fully answered.

e. It is a familiar fact that the apparent size of an object decreases with its increased distance from the eye, but the term apparent size is really a little ambiguous, on account of the interference of knowledge with sense impressions. Thus, when I see a whole house through one window pane, I perceive that the apparent size of the house is less than that of the pane, and it is so because the image of the house on the retina of the eye, which is what determines its *real apparent size to simple sense*, is less than that of the pane. But I *know* that the house is much larger than many panes, and this knowledge is so far controlling, that the sight of the house affords a *mental impression* of an object much larger than the pane, though the merely *sense impression* is, that it is smaller.

In relation to the distinction here explained, a completely natural artist is one, who sees things, only, and just as his sense of sight sees, without any interference from thought or knowledge of *real* relative sizes; and who draws objects just as his eye sees them.

Such a one will spontaneously conform to the principles of perspective, which, in relation to him, will only be the natural history of his natural performances. In proportion, however, as knowledge of the *real* sizes of objects warps the judgment, as to their real *apparent* size to the eye alone, does a scientific knowledge and practice of perspective become necessary as a guard against errors in drawing.

f. According to (14–16) and all the preceding constructions, a perspective drawing should be viewed from the precise point from which the object represented is supposed to be viewed. Thus, Fig. 47 should be viewed by the eye placed in a *perpendicular to the paper at* E, and five inches (= CD) from that point. The perspective will then make identically the same image on the retina that would be made by the original object in its full size, and 25 ft. (the distance by scale) from n, on the perpendicular AnC.

In a picture, properly so called, where the sensible effect is greatly assisted by shade and color, if it be viewed through a tube, so as to exclude the surrounding objects which warp the judgment when compared with the small size of the picture, the illusion may be made complete, by abandoning the mind to the picture exclu sively, and we *really* seem to look up through extended valleys, winding among great hills, and overhung by a real far distant sky.

g. The principal exception to this rule for the position of the eye, is in viewing decorative wall paintings of interiors, which may be painted as if seen from a great distance, or otherwise modified so as not to be offensively distorted to beholders in any ordinary position within the building.

h. In connexion with oblique vision of an object, as mentioned in (*c*), the question occurs, "to what extent is such vision admissi ble." In other words, what is the practical limit of the visual angle. We can examine objects with the greatest minuteness only a point at a time or in the line of but a single visual ray at a time. On the other hand, we can be conscious of the existence of objects within a range of 180°, either vertically or horizontally. Where, now, between these limits, is the greatest visual angle which will allow of a clear and pleasing general effect? It is usually supposed to vary from 45° to 60°.

Accordingly, in Fig. 47, by laying off five inches, = CD, in front of *n*, to obtain the station point (113) (115), and from this point drawing lines to P and E, it will appear that a small visual angle is formed. Hence when Fig. 47 is viewed, as directed in (*f*), it will be very clearly seen.

i. This clear view is also due to looking directly, in the line CA, at the centre of the object. Thus Fig. 47 is much more satisfactory than Figs. 16 and 17, PART I., where the eye is placed considerably to one side of the given object, partly to avoid the confounding of plans and perspectives, and partly to avoid the very acute intersec tions of lines of construction that would have occurred had the point EE' been placed directly in front of the objects.

The last consideration points to another disadvantage of the method of visual rays, especially as employed in connection with two planes only.

EXAMPLE 5.—**To find the Perspective of a Cross and Pedestal.**

This problem is chosen as one embracing numerous lines arranged in parallel sets.

In Fig. 49, let ABD be the plan of the pedestal, EFG, of

the horizontal arm of the cross, and HIIK, that of its vertical arm.

LL is the ground line which indicates the first, and L'L' the one which indicates the second position of the perspective plane. VV' is the level of the eye, and therefore by (105) contains the vanishing points of all the horizontal lines of the object. S is the station point (113) taken in a perpendicular to the perspective plane through the centre of the object (122c).

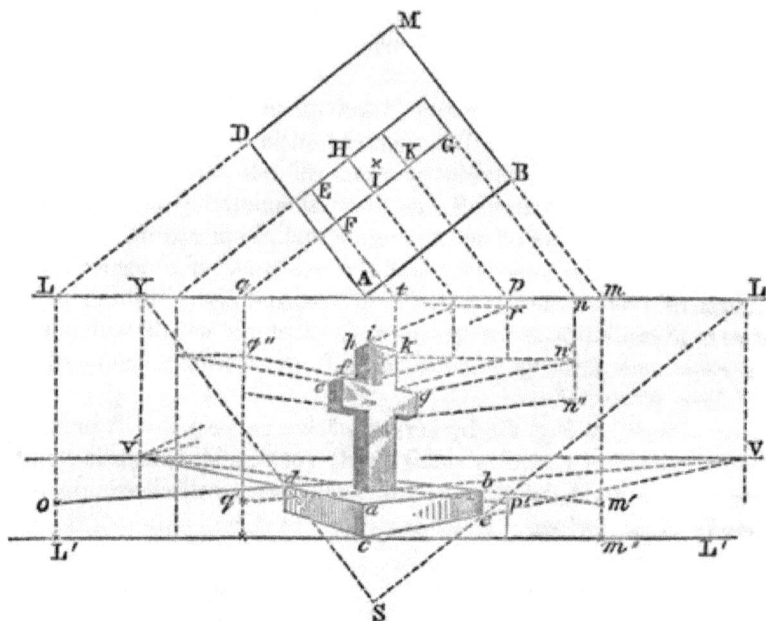

Fig. 49.

Then, drawing SL, parallel to AB, and LV perpendicular to LL, we find V, the vanishing point of all lines in the direction of AB. In a similar manner V' is found. Other points in the indefinite perspectives of the horizontal lines, are where those lines pierce the perspective plane.

Accordingly, as shown by the figure, and (122a) and assuming ca as the height of the pedestal, MB, produced, meets the perspective plane at m', where m'm'' = ac ; and BA meets the perspective plane at a. Then m'V' is the indefinite perspective of BM, and aV, that of AB. Hence b, their intersection, is the perspective of B. From b, draw be, perpendicular to the ground line and limited by cV, and one face of the pedestal will be represented. The construction of its other visible surfaces is similar to the foregoing, as is seen in the figure.

To find the foot of the vertical arm. Kp and Kq pierce the perspective plane at p' and q', at heights equal to ac. p'V$'$ and q'V are their perspectives, which intersect at the perspective of K in the foot of this arm. Other like points are similarly found. On either of the same perpendiculars through p and q, set off the height, as at r, of the whole cross and pedestal, then rV$'$, the perspective of pK in the level of the head of the arm, will meet the right hand edge at k, the perspective of the top point, K.

To find points in the perspective of the short arm EG. Produce its horizontal edges to the ground line, as at q and n. Set off, as before, the heights of these points, as at q'' and n' in the plane of the top of this arm. Then g, for example, the intersection of q''V and n'V$'$, will be the perspective of G. Other points may be similarly found.

Remarks.—*a.* It is evident from this problem that the method by *horizontal* lines of the object, when such exist, is as convenient in respect to avoiding the necessity of full vertical projections, as is the method of diagonals and perpendiculars.

b. The intersection at b, for example, is very acute, but would have been less so had a perpendicular, through B, been used, together with aV. Thus, by an adaptation of auxiliary lines to the conditions of each point, we can obtain the perspective of each by a well defined intersection.

c. The passing of SL through c, and of SY through d, are merely accidental coincidences, which are always liable to occur, but which never need perplex the draftsman if he will retain a clear view of first principles, and keep in mind what each line of the figure really means.

CHAPTER II.

PERSPECTIVES OF SHADOWS.

123. Returning to Fig. 35, PART I., where BR represents a ray of light and AR, its horizontal projection (96), it is evident that R, the shadow of B on the horizontal plane, is the intersection of the ray through B, with its horizontal projection.

It follows, now, that the *perspective* of R will be the intersection of the *perspective* of the ray with the *perspective* of its horizontal projection (117).

If, then, we can find these latter lines, we can find the *perspective* of the shadow directly, or without finding its projections.

124. But rays of light, proceeding, as usually supposed, from the sun, are parallel; hence their vanishing point, like that of other parallels, is found by determining where a parallel ray of light through the point of sight pierces the perspective plane (108). Also, rays being parallel, their projections on either plane will be parallel (53). Their vertical projections, being lines in the perspective plane, will be their own perspectives; and their horizontal projections, being horizontal lines, will have a vanishing point in the horizon (105). Hence the perspectives of rays, and of their horizontal projections, can be found; and therefore *perspectives of shadows on the horizontal plane, can be found directly*, or without previously finding the projections of those shadows, as in PART I.

The principle just established, combined with other general elementary principles already employed, will also, as will soon appear, enable us to find, directly, all ordinary shadows.

We proceed next to illustrate the principles just explained, in some elementary constructions.

EXAMPLE 6.—To find the vanishing point of given Rays, and of their Horizontal Projections.

Let R and R', Fig. 50, be the two projections of a ray of light, which lies in front of the perspective plane, GL being the ground line. Also, let EE' be the point of sight. Then E*h*, parallel to R, and E'V, parallel to R', are the projections of a *visual* ray parallel to the *rays of light*. This visual ray meets the perspective plane in the point whose horizontal projection is h, and whose vertical projection, or the point itself, is V (58). Hence V is the *vanishing point of all rays of light* parallel to R–R'.

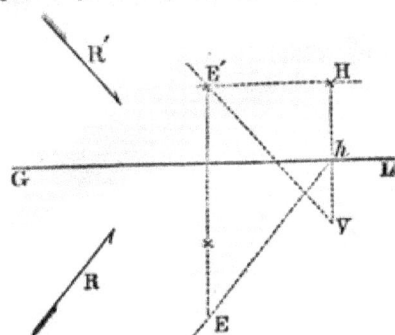

Fig. 50.

Again, remembering that the vertical projection of a horizontal line, oblique to the vertical plane, is a line parallel to the ground line (51) Eh, again, parallel to R, and E'H, parallel to GL, are the projections of a *visual* ray, parallel to the *horizontal projections of the rays of light.* This visual ray pierces the vertical or perspective plane at H, which is therefore the *vanishing point of horizontal projections of rays*, and is in the horizon E'H.

125. Having completed Fig. 50, observe that H and V, are, by construction, *necessarily in the same perpendicular to the ground line.* This follows from the fact that a ray, and its horizontal projection, are in the same vertical plane (81), and therefore the visual rays, as Eh–E'V, and Eh–E'H, parallel to them, are in a vertical plane ; while the vertical trace of such a plane, in which these visual rays pierce the vertical plane of projection, is a line perpendicular to the ground line (79).

126. In general, if a ray, or any other line, be contained in a certain plane, it must pierce any surface in the intersection of the plane with that surface ; that is, in the trace of the plane upon that surface.

127. When a particular direction of the light *is given*, as at R–R', H and V *must be constructed* by (Ex. 6), but if, as is usual in general problems, its direction *is not given*, H and V *may be assumed*, agreeably to (125).

EXAMPLE 7.—To find the **Perspective of the Shadow** of any **Vertical Line** upon the Horizontal Plane.

Let B'L, Fig. 51, be the ground line ; which, in figures of so few lines as Figs. 50 and 51, and similar ones, need not be translated. Let A be the horizontal, and A'B' the vertical projection of the given vertical line. Its perspective, ab, is found by visual rays, as AE—A'E', as explained in PART I., EE' being the point of sight.

Then, by (125) assume V and H, as the vanishing points of rays and horizontal projections of rays, respectively. Then aV is the perspective of the ray of light through the point whose perspective is a, that is through A A', and bH is the perspective of the

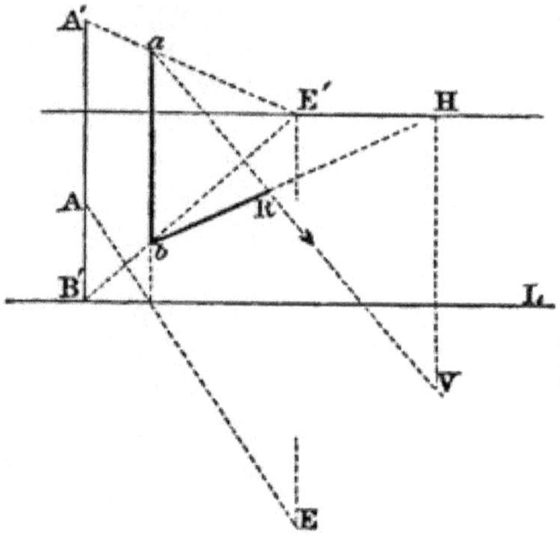

FIG. 51.

horizontal projection of the same ray. Hence by (123) R is the perspective of the shadow of a upon the horizontal plane; and bR is the perspective shadow of ab on the same plane.

Remarks.—*a.* Remembering that when the rays are parallel, as here supposed, they, and their horizontal projections, will, each, have a common vanishing point, it is evident, that if the shadows of a number of vertical lines, like ab, be found on the same horizontal plane, they will all converge to the point H. The student should make this construction.

b. When the vanishing point V is below the horizon, and the light proceeds as indicated by the arrow in Fig. 51, it shows that the light proceeds from above and behind the left shoulder. If V were above H, it would indicate that the light proceeded from above and in front of the right shoulder; and the shadows would fall towards the observer and to the left, as will readily appear on making the construction.

c. If the source of light were a near point, as a candle, the perspective of this point and of its horizontal projection must be found. Lines from the former to points in the perspective object will be the perspectives of rays; and lines from the latter point to the perspectives of horizontal projections of the same points of the object, will be the perspectives of horizontal projections of rays.

Rays from such a luminous point diverge in every direction, hence if in Fig. 51, we suppose AA' to be the luminous point, a is its perspective; and, not aV only, but *any* line from a will be the perspective of some ray.

The completion of the construction thus far explained, is left as an exercise for the student.

CHAPTER III.

128. The following problems are added, not to illustrate any new principles, but to familiarize the student more fully with the application of those already explained, to practical problems.

Premising that the drawing of exterior and interior views of buildings, with their accompaniments; arcades, pavements, and furniture, is perhaps the chief *exact* application of perspective, this chapter is occupied with examples of this character, the execution of which will enable the draftsman to proceed with the perspective drawing of Avenues, Bridges, Machines, etc., and with the correct additions of features of natural scenery to the geometrical portions of his drawings.

EXAMPLE 8.—**To find the Perspective of a Pavement of Squares, whose sides are parallel to the ground line.**

Let GB, Fig. 52, be the ground line, DC the horizontal line, or horizon, and AGK a group of twelve squares, lying in the horizontal plane, and with one side, GK, taken as the ground line.

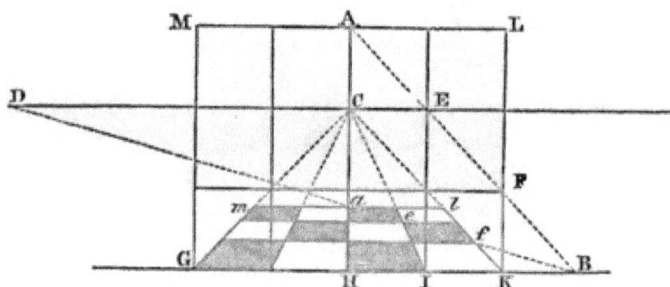

FIG. 52.

Operating by the method of diagonals and perpendiculars, let C be the centre of the picture (113) and D the vanishing point of diagonals. C is the vanishing point of perpendiculars (112) and these perpendiculars, as LK, AH, etc., pierce the perspective plane at K, H, etc., hence (116) KC, HC, etc., are their perspectives. AB is the diagonal from A and BD is its perspective. Therefore a is the perspective of A. Likewise e is the perspective of E, and f, of F. Drawing parallels to GK, through a, e, and f, (111) they will inter-

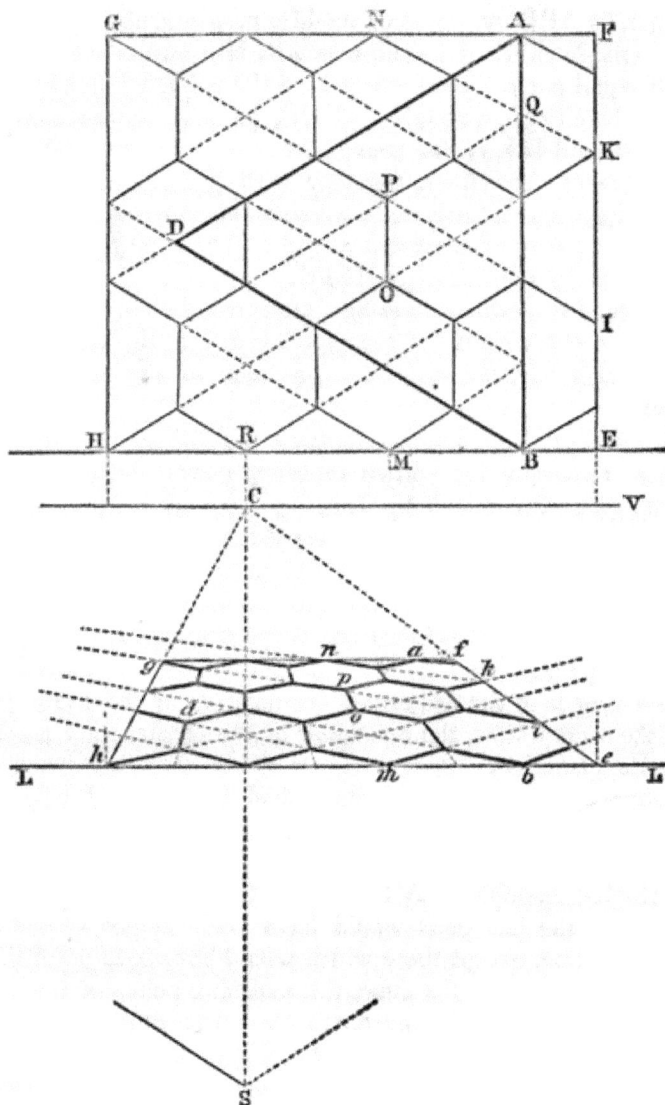

Fig. 53.

sect the perspectives of the perpendiculars, so as to complete the required perspective GmIK.

EXAMPLE 9.—To find the Perspective of a Pavement of Hexagons, whose sides make angles of 30° and 90° with the ground line.

Let HE be the ground line, Fig. 53. Construct an equilateral triangle, as ABD, with one of its sides perpendicular to the ground line. Divide either of its sides, as AB, into any convenient number of equal parts. Through each of the points of division, as Q, draw indefinite lines, as QN and QP, parallel to the remaining sides, DB and DA, of the triangle.

Portions of these lines, together with perpendiculars, as OP, joining the proper intersections, which will be obvious on inspection, will form a group of regular hexagons. These may be limited at pleasure, as by the rectangle HEFG.

Now let LL be the ground line, after translation, CV the horizontal line, C the centre of the picture, and S the station point, taken in this case, for variety, at one side of the middle of the figure.

The sides of the hexagons, forming parallel groups, are taken as lines of construction. Their vanishing points—beyond the limits of the figure—are found by drawing lines at S (partly shown) parallel to HK and IG, till they meet HE. From the latter points, perpendiculars to CV produced, will meet CV in the vanishing points of HK and IG and of all lines parallel to them. The remaining lines of the hexagons are perpendiculars, and C is their vanishing point.

Observing that the plans and perspectives of the same points have the same letters, the remainder of the construction needs no further explanation.

Remark. If, in Ex. 8, the squares had been placed with their sides making angles of 45° with the ground line, those sides would all have been diagonals, instead of parallels and perpendiculars.

In the last example, if AB had been taken in the ground line, the sides of the hexagons would have made angles of 60° with the ground line, except those which would have been parallel to it. Hence, SR remaining the same, the vanishing points of the inclined sides would have been nearer to C. The student should reconstruct these examples under these new conditions.

EXAMPLE 10.—To find the Perspective of an Interior.

Preliminary explanation. According to (122h) a person standing against one wall of a room, can be conscious of the entire interior, though the whole cannot be distinctly recognized. If, then, Fig. 54, a person stand at E, seeing clearly everything within the

visual angle AEB, only the portion of the room beyond AB can be represented in a picture. Hence, if a larger portion, or the whole of the interior is to be represented, the near wall A'B" must be supposed to be removed, so that E', or E", may be the position of the observer, from which all beyond A'B', or A"B", will be visible.

Construction of Fig. 55. In this example, let the near wall be removed, and let the whole interior be seen under a visual angle of 45°. ABGL is

Fig. 54.

the plan of the room, with an elliptically arched passage, of the width EF, opening out of it on the right, and with a door, HK, in the left wall.

Let the observer stand opposite the point X, at one third the width of the room from G. We have then to construct S, the vertex of an angle of 45°, whose base is GL, and placed opposite to X. Draw GT and LT, each making an angle of 45° with GL. Draw, at X, a perpendicular to GL, and with T as a centre and TG as a radius, describe a small arc, intersecting this perpendicular at S, which will be the station point as required.

Now let G'L' be the ground line, indicating the second position of the perspective plane, and let CD be the horizontal line. This line must, if the observer is supposed to stand on the floor, be about *five feet* above G'L', on the same scale on which the plan, AG, is drawn. Note that C is in the perpendicular XS, produced to meet CD.

Observing, now, that a diagonal from A will meet LG at a distance to the left of L, equal to LA, and so for other points, the diagonals themselves need not be drawn. Thus, make CD = SX (115) and D will be a vanishing point of diagonals. Then make L'A = LA and A'D will be the perspective of the diagonal from A. The perspective of the perpendicular LA is L'C, hence α is the perspective of the right hand back corner, A, of the floor. Draw *ab*, parallel to L'G', till it meets G'C, the perspective of GB, and L'G' *ab* will be the perspective of the floor.

The front wall of the room, GL, being taken as the perspective plane, the intersection of the room with that plane will be its own perspective, in full size and real form. Hence make L'L" and G'G" equal to the height of the walls; and, supposing the ceiling to be semicircular, describe a semicircle on L"G" as a diameter.

As an example of a simple cornice, in perspective, make the small rectangles at L" and G", as sections of it in the perspective

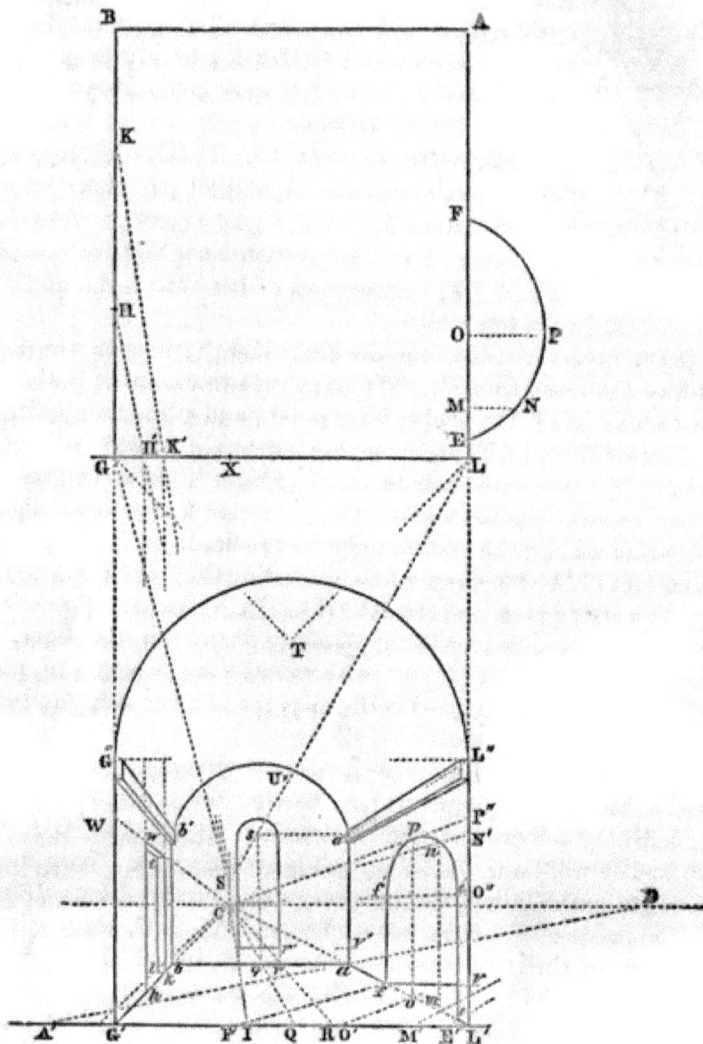

Fig. 55.

plane. Then draw its edges towards C, limiting it by a horizontal and vertical line where its lower back edge, on each wall, meets the vertical lines from *a* and *b*.

QC is the perspective of a perpendicular through the centre of the floor. Hence *qs* is the perspective of the centre line of the further wall. Where *qs* meets *a′s*, *a′* being the intersection of *aa′* nd L″C, is the centre of the semicircular boundary of the further end of the ceiling; which is a semicircle in perspective, because it is parallel to the perspective plane. If there be a round topped window in the centre of the further wall, lay off its half width, QR=QI, each side of the middle point Q, draw RC and IC, and perpendiculars to *ab* as at *r*. Then make L′v equal to the height of the base above the floor, draw *v*C, and *v′r′* paralled to *ab*, and the semicircular top, with *s* as a centre, to have it concentric with the ceiling. This will complete the outline of the window.

To draw the opening HK (which is very wide in order to show the construction more plainly). Draw HS and KS, horizontal projections of visual rays, or horizontal traces of *vertical visual planes*, through the sides of the opening. Then the intersections of these planes with the perspective plane, at *hw* and *k*, drawn from H′ and K′, will be the perspectives of the vertical doorway lines at H and K. Make G′W equal to the height of the door, and WC will limit the inside of the top of the door. Next draw the edges in the thickness of the doorway as *kl*, parallel to G′L′, the vertical line *lt*, and from *t* the line towards C, which completes the doorway.

To draw the archway EF. Make L′E′=LE, and L′F′=LF. Draw E′D and F′D, which will give *e* and *f*, the perspectives of E and F. Make L′O″ equal to the height of the vertical portion of the archway, and limit the vertical lines at *e* and *f*, by O″C. To find the perspective of the highest point, draw the semi-ellipse, FPE, representing the elliptical top of the arch as revolved round EF, till parallel to the horizontal plane. Lines, as OP, in this semi-ellipse, are called ordinates. Take the longest ordinate, OP, set it off at O″P′ and draw P″C. Make L′O′=LO, draw O′D, and *op*, then *p* will be the perspective of O, that is of P. Any point in the ellipse may be similarly found. Thus, take MN any where, and parallel to OP. Make O″N′=MN, and draw N′C. Also make L′M′=LM, draw M′D and *mn*, then *n*, the intersection of *mn* with N′C, will be the perspective of N. After finding one or two more points in like manner, the perspective ellipse, *f′pne′* can be sketched. The horizontal line at *f* will then complete the archway, and the whole figure.

EXAMPLE 11.—To find the Perspectives of the Shadows in an Interior.

In order not to confuse figure 55, the constructions of the required shadows are made on the following enlarged copies of detached portions.

First ; to find the shadow of the edges of the doorway, Fig. 56. Supposing no particular direction of the light to be given, assume H as the vanishing point of horizontal projections of rays, and R,

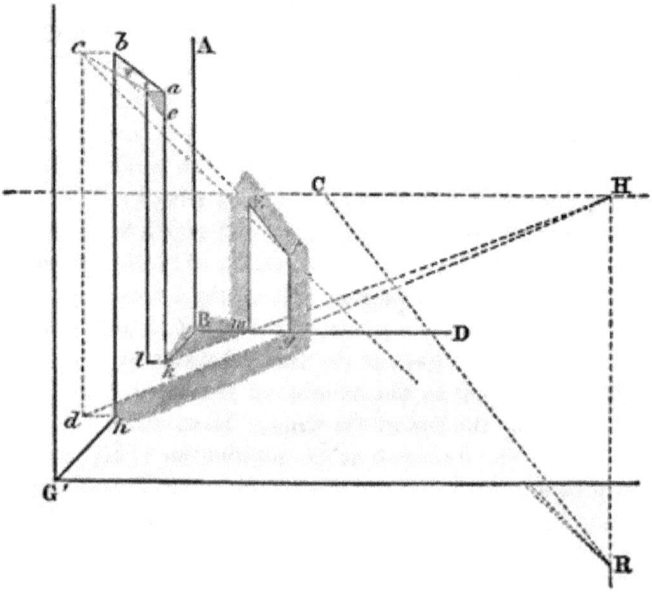

FIG. 56.

as the vanishing point of rays. It is readily apparent on consideration, that *ka*, *tc* and *cd* are those edges of the doorway, parts of which, at least, will cast shadows. *k*H is the perspective of the horizontal projection of all rays through the vertical edge *ka*. That is, it is the horizontal trace of a vertical plane of rays (99) through *ka*. It is therefore the shadow of *ka* on the floor, as far as *m*, where it meets the further wall ABD. Thence, this plane being vertical, its trace, and shadow of *ka* on ABD, is vertical, as seen at *m*E.

To find E, consider that *ct* will partly cast a shadow on the surface *atk*. This surface being parallel to the perspective plane, and *ct* perpendicular to it, the shadow of *ct* on *atk* will be parallel to the vertical projection, CR, of a ray of light (97), and will begin at t, where ct meets atk. Hence te, parallel to CR (111) is the shadow of ct on atk. Therefore e is the highest point of ka that can cast a shadow. Hence draw the ray eR, and E, its intersection with mE, will be the limit of the shadow of ka. The remainder of the construction is now evident from the figure.

Since light streams through the doorway, the area within th shadow of its edges is light, as indicated by the partial shade line of the figure.

Second. To find the shadow in the archway, Fig. 57. This shadow is in four parts; first, the shadow of the edge ee' upon the floor; second, that of the same edge on the wall Gff'; third, that of the curve $e'pf'$ on the same wall; and fourth, that of the same curve upon the cylindrical surface of the archway, above the horizontal plane through e' and f'.

Let H be the vanishing point of horizontal projections of rays, and R, the vanishing point of rays. Then eH is the perspective of

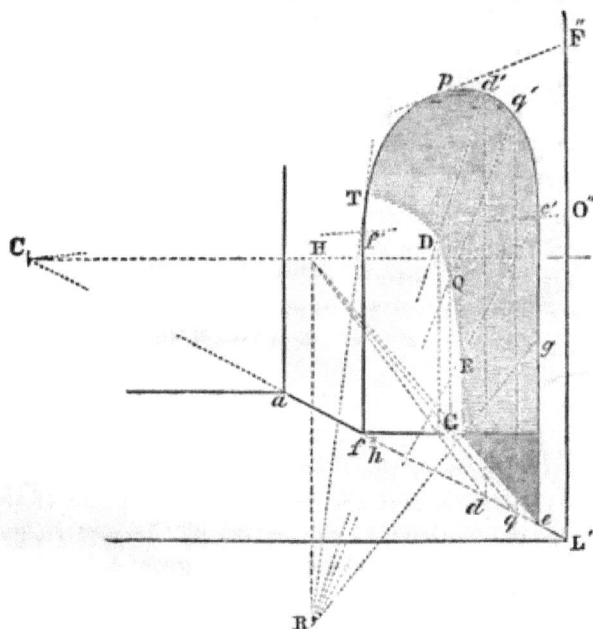

Fig. 57.

the horizontal trace of a vertical plane of rays through ee', and eG is the shadow of this edge on the floor. By drawing the ray RG, and producing it to g, we learn that eg is the precise portion of ee' which casts a shadow on the floor. From G, the shadow of ge' is the vertical line GE, limited at E by the ray e'R. Above E, the shadow is cast by the arch curve, and is found as follows. Assume any point, q', and draw the vertical line $q'q$, which is the trace of a vertical plane of rays through q', upon the side of the room. Then qH is the perspective of the trace of this plane upon the floor, and the vertical line from the intersection of qH with fG, is its trace on the wall of the arch. This plane contains the ray q'R, which meets the vertical line, just named, at Q, which is therefore the shadow of q'. D, the shadow of d' is found in like manner. T, the point of contact of the ray TR, with the arch curve fpe', is the upper end of the shadow, which may be sketched by joining the points already found.

In this figure, the shadow on the cylindrical surface of the arch is so small, that no points in it have been found, except T. The most elementary method of finding points of this shadow, is the following indirect one, which is so fully indicated that the student will probably find no difficulty in applying it for himself. Assume any point as h quite near to f, on $L'a$, and draw through it lines parallel to fG and ff', which will represent a plane parallel to the wall Gff. This plane will cut a line from the arch, parallel to fG, and beginning where the vertical line from h meets the arch curve. Next find a few points of shadow on this plane, just as DQE was found. Then the intersection of this auxiliary shadow with the horizontal line cut from the arch, will be a point of shadow on the arch (99) and by drawing a ray from R through this point, we can find the precise point on fpe' which casts this point of shadow.

EXAMPLE 12.—**To find the Perspective of a Cabin.**

In this example, a variety of methods will be employed, by way of review; also some special operations, suited to the construction of particular points.

Let ABD, Fig. 58, be the plan of the cabin walls, EF of its roof ridge, and H″HI of its chimney. Let the perspective plane be taken at GK, through the corner A, and let G′K′ be its ground line after translation and revolution into the plane of the paper. Let VV′ be the horizon, C the centre of the picture, and S the station point. The perpendicular to the ground line, and containing S and C passes through *, the centre of the plan (122 i).

The edge at A, being in the perspective plane, is its own perspective, and appears in its real height at aa'. The visual ray BS—L′C pierces the perspective plane at b, the perspective of the lower corner at B. Make L″B″$=aa'$, then BS—B″C is the visual ray from the upper corner at B, and b' is the perspective of that corner. Draw ab and $a'b'$.

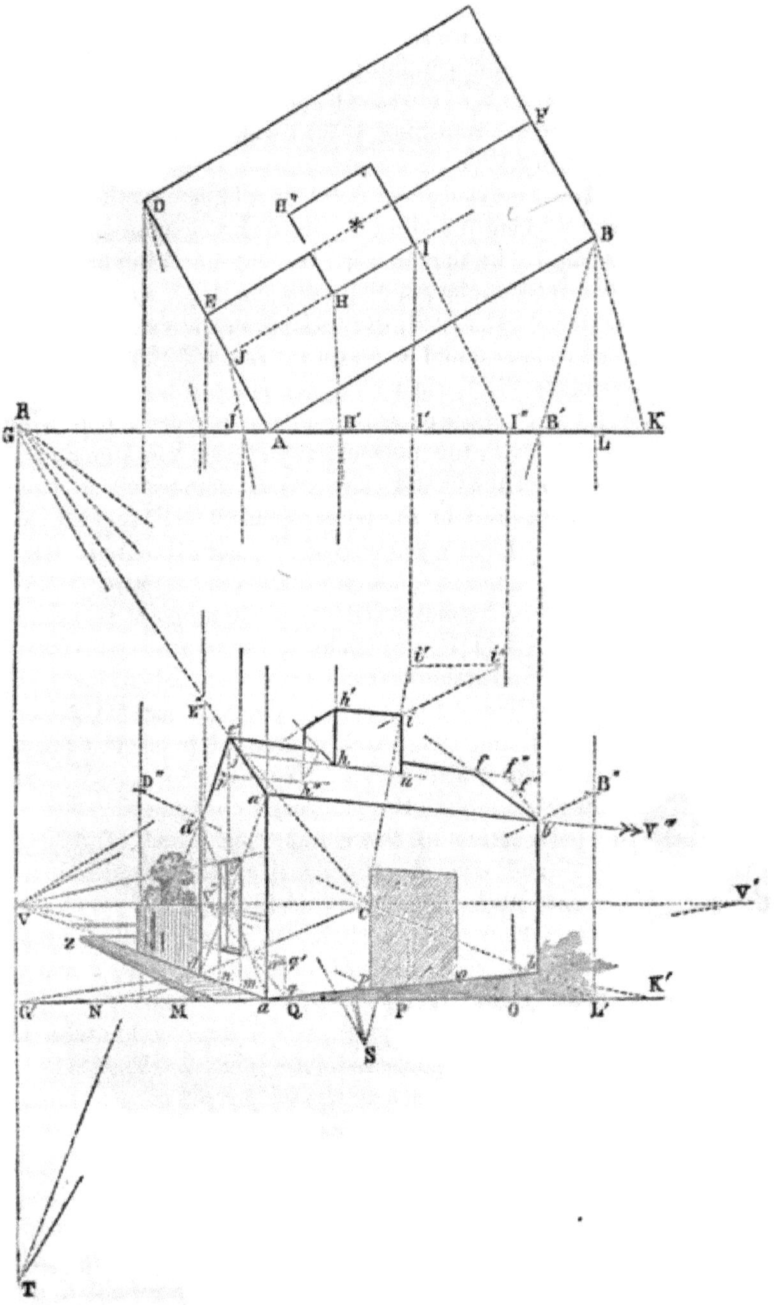

FIG. 58.

The vanishing point of all lines parallel to AB, can now be found in either of two ways. In the usual way, it would be found by drawing through S a line parallel to AB, till it meets GK, whence drop a perpendicular to VV' (108). Or, produce ab and $a'b'$ till they meet VV', in the same vanishing point; which, being out of the paper, is indicated by V'''.

Likewise find V, the vanishing point of all lines parallel to AD, in the usual way, if before finding dd', or as just explained, if after finding dd', as shown in the figure. Having found the end, add', of the cabin, the intersection, e, of its diagonals ad' and da', is the perspective centre of that end, over which, in the vertical line ee', the peak of the roof is found as follows. Lay off the real height, projected from E, at E''; then E''C, the perspective of a perpendicular from E, will intersect ee' at e', the perspective of EE''. Now draw $a'e'$ and $d'e'$, the perspectives of the left end lines of the roof. These lines are in the same vertical plane with ad, hence their vanishing points are in the perpendicular, GG', to G'K' and through V (125-6). Hence produce $a'e'$ to meet GG' in R, which will be the vanishing point of all lines parallel, in space, to $a'e'$. Also $e'd'$, produced to T, makes T the vanishing point of all lines parallel to $e'd'$. To find R and T by the usual process, consider that $a'E''$ and $D'E''$ are the vertical projections of AE and DE, and then find where lines through the point of sight C, S, and parallel to $a'E''$—AE and $D'E''$—DE, pierce the perspective plane, which will be, as before, at R and T. Next draw $e'f$ to V''', and $b'f$ to R, which will complete the perspective of the roof.

To find the perspective of the chimney, and first of its base. Produce IH to J and, drawing the visual ray JS, project J' into the edge of the roof at j. Then draw jh through V'''; or, by elementary geometry, draw $b'f''$ parallel to $a'e'$, and limit it by $e'f$ produced, then divide $a'e'$ and $b'f''$ proportionally at j and f' and draw jf' (For example, if $e'j$ is $\frac{1}{4}$ of $e'a'$, then make $f''f'=\frac{1}{4}$ of $e''b'$). Find h by the visual ray HS, whose intersection with the perspective plane at H' is projected into jf' at h. Find u in the same way from I. To find i, set up the full height of the chimney top from the ground at i', projected from I, and draw the perspective perpendicular i'C to limit the vertical edge ui at i. Other wise: (Ex. 5.) produce the right hand side of the chimney to I', and set up its height, projected from I', at i'', and limit ui by i''V. Then limit hh' by ih' drawn through V''', and draw h'V. Draw hR until the ridge is met, thence a line towards T, limited as follows. Draw jV and note j', its intersection with $e'd'$, whence draw a line, $j'h'$, to V''', limiting an edge of the chimney at h'', whence draw this edge, which is limited by $h'V$.

In finding the door and window, further special constructions will be used, as proposed.

If lines be drawn, parallel to any line as BK, AB and AK will be similarly, that is, proportionally divided, and if AK=AB, these similar parts will be equal, and in the same order. Hence make aK'=AB, and $K'b$ will be the perspective of KB, and V'', its intersection with VV', will be the vanishing point of all parallels to KB, (106). Then make aP and aO equal to the distances of the two sides of the door from a, that is from A, and draw PV'' and OV'' which will meet ab at p and o, the perspectives of the sides of the threshold. Set off the true height of the door from a on aa' and draw a line to V'', which will complete the door by limiting the verticals at p and o.

In like manner, a window in the front of the cabin could be put in perspective.

To find the perspective of the end window. According to the method just explained, make aG'=AD (G' accidentally falls on the perpendicular RT (Ex. 5. *Rem. c.*) and let NM be the true relative width and place of the window. Draw $G'dV'$, analogous to $K'b$, also NV' and MV'. At n and m draw vertical lines, and having made aa'' equal to the height of the window seat, limit them by $a''V$. Make aQ equal to the thickness of the cabin wall, and draw QV'', noting q, its intersection with ab. Then draw qq', limited by $a''V''$, and from q' draw $q'V$, which gives the inner edge of the window seat. From the further upper and lower outer corners of the window, short lines are seen, which being perpendicular to the end wall, are parallel to ab, and therefore vanish at V'''. The lower one of these lines is limited by $q'V$, and from the point thus given, the inner vertical line of the window is drawn, which at y limits the upper line to V''', and the inner top line which vanishes at V.

The horizontal lines of the fence and sidewalk vanish at V. The top of the fence being in the line VC, it is thus shown to be about five feet high. At Z is shown a fragment of a cross street, parallel to the perspective plane. The *real* distance of this street from a, or A, is equal to the distance from a to the intersection of $V'Z$ produced (not shown) with aG' produced. The tree in the yard is seen, by comparing with the top line of the window, to be about twelve feet high.

129. By comparison of Fig. 58, with **any** of those in PART I., it

appears, on inspection, that the *perspective*, as L'C, *of a perpendi*
cular, is the same as the *vertical projection*, L'C, *of a visual ray*,
BS—L'C, though the same point. This is evident from the
definitions of these lines. Each, it will be seen, joins the vertical
projection of the point through which it passes, with the vertical
projection of the point of sight, which latter is the centre of the
icture.

EXAMPLE 13.—**To find the Perspective of the Shadow of
a Chimney on a Roof.**

Fig. 59 is substantially an enlarged copy of a part of the roof of
Fig. 58, but with the proportions, and the level of the eye, changed,
merely to bring the construction within the limits of the page. H,

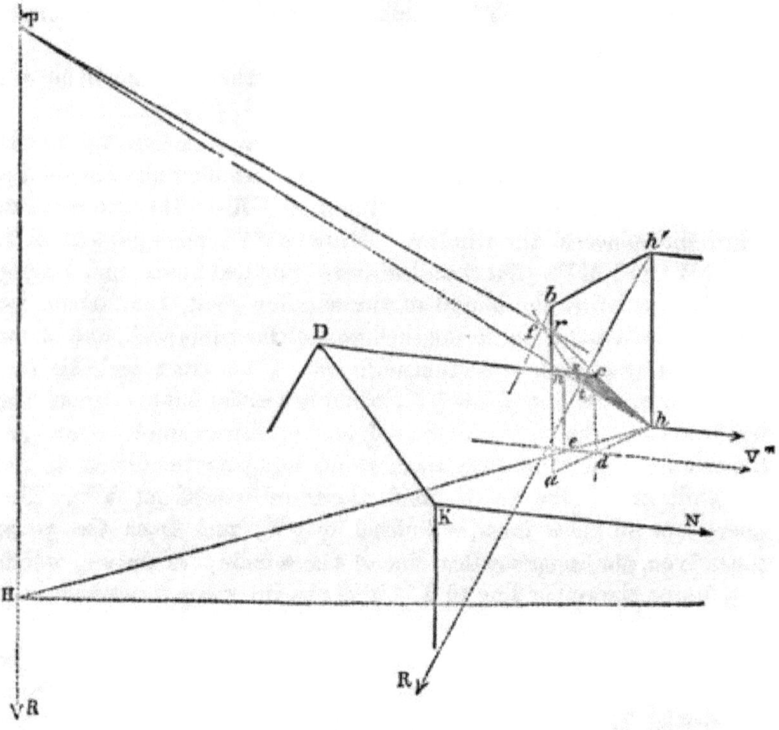

FIG. 59.

in the horizontal line, is the vanishing point of projections of rays
on any horizontal plane (Ex. 6). R, on HR, but not shown in its
real position, is the vanishing point of rays.

Now to find the shadow of the edge *hh'* upon the roof. This shadow will be the trace on the roof, of a vertical plane of rays through hh'. The line ah, joining the intersections of the edges of the chimney with the roof, is horizontal in space, and in the side surface of the chimney, within the roof. cd is a line in a vertical plane through the ridge Dc, and is also in the same side of the chimney. Hence dV''', drawn to V''' (see Fig. 58.) is the trace of the central vertical plane, through Dc, upon the horizontal plan through ah. Now hH is the perspective or the trace of a plane of rays through hh' upon the latter plane; en, a vertical line from the intersection of hH with dV''', and meeting the ridge Dc at n, is the trace of the same plane of rays on the vertical plane through Dc. Hence nh is the trace of the plane of rays upon the roof. The ray $h'R$, in this plane, meets this trace at t, which is therefore the shadow of h'. Hence th is the shadow of hh'. A portion of the shadow of $h'b$ is visible, which is found as follows. Produce hc to meet ab in r, which is therefore the intersection of ab with the front side of the roof, produced. Next, produce hn to T in the perpendicular RHT, and T will be the vanishing point of all traces of vertical planes of rays on the front roof. Hence Tr is the perspective trace of a vertical plane of rays through ab upon the indefinite plane of the front of the roof. Drawing the ray bR, it gives f as the shadow of b upon the front roof produced. Hence ft is the shadow of bh' on this roof, and the portion, st, of this shadow is real, and visible.

Remark. In concluding these examples of shadows, and of this volume, it may be added, that though few, the student will find them so varied, that, by attentively considering them, he will doubtless be able to construct any ordinary shadow, or at least to judge more accurately of the appearance of shadows, sketched directly or without construction.

CHAPTER IV.

PICTURES, AND AERIAL PERSPECTIVE.

130. For full instructions on the subject of this chapter, those who make perspective drawings, primarily for pictorial effect, should consult books which treat of perspective as an imitative art (27). A few topics only are here treated, principally for the information of those who may have occasion to add a few subordinate items of scenery, &c., to drawings mainly of a geometrical character.

131. *Landscape outlines.* These, to be sketched in their true *apparent* position and form, must be seen with truly artistic or childlike sense, that is, without interference by the knowledge of their *real* position and form. In other words, we simply copy what the eye sees, and just as it sees it, and *not* what the *mind infers* from what the *eye sees* (122 e).

132. In proportion as we abandon reliance on simple sense, for scientific knowledge, will the unassisted eye fail to serve us perfectly ; and some mechanical guide to it will become necessary or convenient.

It would be impracticable, however, to make preliminary plans and elevations of broad landscape areas, such as have been employed in the preceding geometrical constructions. Hence simpler aids are sought. Among these is the use of a *pencil and string*, as a measure of relative apparent sizes and spaces. Thus, if one end of a cord of fixed length be held in the teeth, and a pencil, attached to the other end of the cord, be always held perpendicularly to the string, the latter being always horizontal, it will be easy to measure on the pencil the apparent dimensions of objects, and the distances and directions of lines between different prominent points in the view to be drawn. After this, the remaining outlines can be sketched by the eye alone.

A more complete guide to the draftsman is a *frame of threads*. Thus, by interposing at a suitable distance, that is, so as to include the whole of a proposed view, a rectangular frame, carrying threads which cross each other at right angles about an inch apart, the actual landscape will be, to the eye, divided into square inches. The paper being then divided into similar squares, all that is seen in each thread square can be accurately located, by reference to its sides, within the corresponding square on the drawing.

133. This last process simplifies picture drawing, by making the whole view consist of the sum of many little pictures, each of which is so small, that by fixing the undivided attention of the eye pon it, it can be drawn just as it is seen, according to (131). By keeping this in mind, and by gradually enlarging the squares, either of the frame alone, or the picture alone, or of both, the eye may be trained into independence of such guides.

134. *Landscape details. Trees.* These, if few, large, and near, and in a real field, yard, or street, may have their position and height indicated in projection, as in the preceding geometrical constructions. Their perspectives will then serve as guides in sketching smaller similar objects. Remote trees will be known as larger than near ones, if they rise higher above the horizon, while standing on the same level. Straight rows of trees may be more accurately drawn, by locating the vanishing point of the line along which they are ranged.

134. *Hills* will be known by their rising above the horizon; and their relative distances, either by the cutting off of their crest lines; or by their height above the horizon, if of equal heights; or by their dimness of color and shade when finished.

Thus in this little sketch, the mountain stream in ascending, flows between the foremost, or right hand hill, and the more remote left hand one, while the dim central peak is evidently distant and quite high.

136. *Valleys,* below the observer's level, will be known by animals, shrubs, &c., in them appearing below the horizon. Also if the descent into them is sudden, they may be plainly indi-

FIG. 60.

cated by the crest of the high ground before them, together with the greater distinctness of the objects shown in the foreground, as in the following sketches; the first a sea view from a precipitous shore, the second a land view of a broad valley seen from near the crest of an elevated table land.

FIG. 61.

FIG. 62.

137. *Ascent and descent* from the observer, is indicated, in land-scape views, by the placing of men, animals, shrubs, rocks, &c., respectively, further and further above, or below the horizon. In street views, the relative direction of the basement and sidewalk lines will show the same thing. Thus in the engraving, V is the vanishing point of horizontal lines, and V′, of the street lines; hence the view is that of a descending street. See also the remote figure, whose eye is below the horizon.

FIG. 63.

In the following figure, however, where V′, the vanishing point of the street lines, is above V, that of the horizontal lines, the street evidently ascends.

138. *Level of the eye.* In interior and street views, particularly, the horizon should not be chosen thoughtlessly, or in improbable positions. In Fig. 64, its position indicates a view taken either from higher ground than that shown in the figure, or from the second story of houses like those on the right, and standing on the level of the line *a*V.

139. *Reflections in water.* Two particulars may here be ncted. *First ;* reflections of the sun and moon on the water should not make an acute angle with the horizon, as is sometimes done, but should be perpendicular to that line, in the picture. The reason is obvious. The incident rays to the water, and the reflected rays from it to the eye, by which the band of light on the water becomes visible, are in a vertical plane. But the intersection of this plane with the perspective plane, is the perspective of this reflection, and this intersection is perpendicular to the horizon (79).

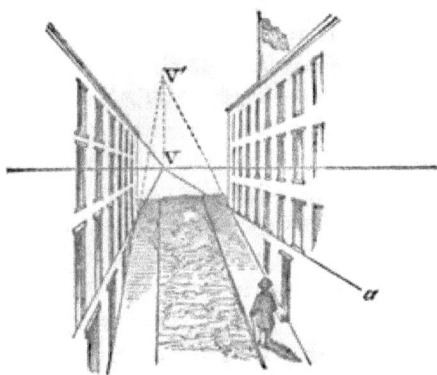

Fig. 64.

Second ; images in the water sometimes show surfaces of an object, not seen directly. Thus in the annexed figure of a wall stand-

Fig. 65.

ing in water, the top of the coping is seen on the wall itself, but the under side in the reflection ; which, being nearest the water, can alone send rays to it to be reflected to the eye.

140. *Location of the centre of the picture.* This point, in order to afford an equally clear view of all parts of the picture, should coincide with the geometrical centre of the drawing. It may be varied slightly from this position, however, in order to show with especial distinctness the more interesting or important parts of the picture. In " bird's eye views," it will be quite above the middle of the canvas.

141. *Location of the perspective plane.* This has, in all the preceding problems, been understood to be between the eye and the object. It is not necessarily so, but is so placed in order, first to reduce, rather than expand any graphical errors in the projections, and, second, to avoid the increased length and confusion of the lines of construction, which would result from having the perspective larger than the projections. It is evident that the latter consequence would follow, for the eye being the vertex of the visual cone, and the apparent contour of the given object its base, then the section of this cone, made by the perspective plane if placed beyond the object, would be larger than that base. That is, the perspective of the object would be larger than its apparent contour. If, then, there is any error in the projections of the object, this error will be magnified in the magnified perspective thus produced.

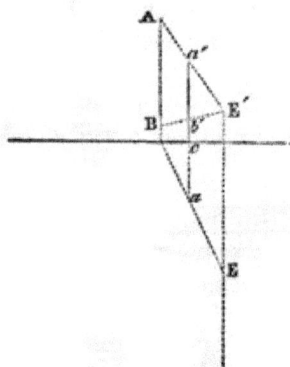

Illustration. See Fig. 66. Let a–a'b' be a vertical line, at the distance ca in front of the perspective plane : and let EE' be the point of sight. Then by (58) the visual ray Ea–E'a' pierces the perspective plane at A, the perspective of aa', and the ray Ea–E'b' pierces it at B, the perspective of ab'. Hence AB is the perspective of a–a'b', and is evidently larger than the latter line.

142. *Shadows of trees, and other vertical objects.* Knowing that these are parallel in fact, when they fall on the same plane, they might, by overlooking Ex. 7, Rem. a be made so in the drawing. They should, however, all converge to one point, so that *in the picture,* shadows of posts, &c., at the right of the vanishing point of rays will incline to the left, while similar shadows on the left of the same point, will incline to the right, when the light comes from behind the observer.

FIG. 66.

143. *Time of a given aspect.* By knowing the direction of vision, the direction of the shadows of vertical lines upon the ground will indicate the part of the day at which a view was taken. Thus, if the direction of the shadows indicates that the vanishing point of rays, R, is to the right and below the centre of the picture, while the observer faces the west, the picture will represent a

morning scene ; or in summer, and in high latitudes, the same position of R would indicate an early morning view to an observer
facing the south. These two cases could be distinguished by th
lengths of the shadows. Also if R were above and to the right of
the eye, the observer looking south, an afternoon view would be
indicated. This is a point of some practical importance in reveal
ng the aspect of dwellings, &c., on proposed sites, at given time
of day.

144. *Light and shade.* The intensity and distribution of shade
upon a body, depends on so many circumstances, and is subject to
so many modifications, that its exact representation in real cases
must be mostly an art of pure imitation. A few points are here
mentioned, as guides to the observations of the student.

1.—The light and shade of a body depends upon its *form.*
Double curved surfaces (87) have a brilliant *point,* or point so
situated as to reflect the most rays to the eye. Plane and single
curved surfaces, have a similar brilliant *line.* On all bodies, the
line, at all points of which rays are tangent to the body, is the
apparently darkest line. Its exact construction, in any given case,
is a problem of practical geometry, of more or less complexity.

2.—Light and shade, depends upon the *nature* of a surface, as
dull or polished. In the former case, the brilliant point is less
intense and is more expanded into an area, while all parts of the
body towards the eye are distinctly visible. In the latter case, the
more perfect the polish, the smaller and more intense the brilliant
point, and the more nearly invisible all the rest of the body, owing
to the absence of reflectinos from it, directed towards the eye.

3.—Light and shade is affected by *distance.* If a surface is *in
the light,* the more *distant* it is, the *darker* it appears, owing to the
extinguishment of the reflected rays from it by the atmosphere,
and floating particles therein. If it be *in the dark,* the more
distant it is, the *lighter* it appears, since we attribute to it the
increased light entering the eye from the greater depth of illu
mined air between us and it.

If, then, a surface be seen obliquely, it will appear gradually
darker as it recedes, if it is in the light ; and gradually lighter as it
recedes, if it is in the dark. Shadows, in like manner, are darkest
where nearest to the objects casting them, and lightest in their
remotest portions.

Hence, at very great distances, the contrast between light and
shade diminishes, as seen in the faint shades and shadows of hills
in the misty distance.

4.°—Light and shade is again affected by the *nature of the light.* A *diffused light*, as on a cloudy day, partially confounds lights and shades in a monotonous uniformity. A *concentrated light*, as on a clear day, affords well defined and vivid contrasts of light and shade.

But again; an *intense light*, as that of the sun, produces reflections so strong as to diminish the contrasts of light and shade, while the black shadows occasioned by the *weaker moonlight* are in familiar contrast with the white lights afforded by it.

145. *Edges.* In shaded drawings, edges are never to be distinguished by black lines. Being really rounded, through imperfection of human instruments, or by attrition or crumbling, they have their own brilliant lines, as cylindrical surfaces, and are distinguished by lighter tints for a minute width. The brilliant lines of edges in the light, are due to primary light falling on them; those of edges in the dark, that is which separate two dark surfaces, to reflected light; and both, to the superior polish acquired in part by the friction of passing particles to which edges are exposed.

Those edges, however, which separate light from shaded *plane* surfaces, are minute cylindrical surfaces so placed as to have a line of shade (144, 1°) upon them, and may be indicated by a line of slightly darker tint than that of the illuminated surface which they bound.

Hence parallel surfaces, near together, should not be distinguished by material differences of tint on their illuminated portions, but by the treatment of their edges, and by the shadows, if any, of the foremost on the one behind it.

146. *The Color of objects* is modified chiefly by the *color of the light* by which they are seen; and by distance, and the condition of the atmosphere. To do justice to the former topic, would lead further into optical discussions than is here proposed. In respect to the latter, we observe, that distance causes all colors to be confounded more and more in the blue of the atmospheric depths through which they are seen.

Trusting that these problems and notes have now been sufficiently extended, to guard the geometrical draftsman from doing offensive violence to artistic truth, and the artist from doing equally offensive violence to geometrical truth, we here terminate both.

REESE LIBRARY
OF THE
UNIVERSITY
OF
CALIFORNIA.

THE END.

www.ingramcontent.com/pod-product-compliance
Lightning Source LLC
Chambersburg PA
CBHW030627270326
41927CB00007B/1337